W9-BXZ-809

Praise for *Heavenly Minded Mom*

"God put this book in my path right when I needed it, at a time when our family was going through a health crisis. Reading it in hospital waiting rooms, I kept thinking about how we function with a small view of life, especially when we're caught in the middle of a struggle. Along comes Katie Bennett. With beauty and grace, she reminds us all what we're really living for: eternity. This book reawakened me to the beauty of my future home, a place called Heaven. I'll be recommending this book to many moms, for years to come."
—**Jennifer Dukes Lee**, author of *The Happiness Dare* and *Love Idol*

"*Heavenly Minded Mom* is a no-fluff, gospel-drenched devotional that will take you to the throne room of the Father. If you've found yourself ever succumbing to the worries of today instead of looking at today in light of eternity (and who of us hasn't?), then you must get your hands on this book. A classic devotional in the making, *Heavenly Minded Mom* is a tool for worship that I will go back to again and again."
—**Erin Odom**, author of *More Than Just Making It* and *You Can Stay Home with Your Kids* and creator of The Humbled Homemaker

"In an age where most devotionals simply 'tickle one's ears,' Katie has successfully delved deep into the heart of the Christian life in short, bite-sized daily readings. I must admit, I am usually wary of this sort of devotional because they are typically shallow and superficial but this devotional you hold in your hand is both thought-provoking and based on God's Word. If you are looking for a resource to help you draw closer to our Creator, to strengthen your resolve to live a gospel-centered life, and to learn how to daily pick up your cross and follow Christ in this modern age, *Heavenly Minded Mom* will indeed remind you that where your treasure is, there your heart is also."
—**Jami Balmet**, blogger at Young Wife's Guide and creator of Homemaking Ministries.com

"There isn't a Christian mother today who wouldn't benefit from the gospel-based, encouraging truths in *Heavenly Minded Mom*. I find myself recalling and rereading Katie's words throughout my day; this book is a true gift. Can't wait to read it with my church Bible study!"
—**Jessica Smartt**, creator of Smartter Each Day

"What a gift *Heavenly Minded Mom* is to those of us looking for ways to keep our focus on things that matter in life and approach our days with the perspective we're meant for—an eternal one. Any mother looking for more meaning and fulfillment in our every day will be hugely blessed by Katie Bennett's scripture-based encouragement and inspiration toward a fuller, God-glorifying life."
—**Jessica Kastner**, author of *Hiding from the Kids in My Prayer Closet* and creator of #UnMom

"Katie has such a heart for pointing moms to Christ, and it's evident in *Heavenly Minded Mom*. This 90-day journey acts as a beacon of truth in our weary world, calling moms to focus on what truly matters. It's filled with deep, insightful thoughts and questions women need to contemplate, but rarely do."
—**Hilary Bernstein**, creator of NoPlaceLikeHomeMedia.com

"Katie's heart for our keeping our eyes on heaven is palpable. She makes me pray and think and move intentionally and grow in so many ways with her encouragement and teaching on eternal perspective. This book, message, and Katie have blessed me, and I can't wait to see how it blesses others."
—**Leah Heffner**, podcaster and blogger at Life Around the Coffee Cup

"As a mom of four young children, this devotional spoke purpose and life into my heart. Every little (and big) task that comes with motherhood can help to shape us into the woman that God has created us to be. Katie has given us a resource that will remind us that we are to live a life that ultimately honors Christ through everything we do. By providing scripture references and real-life examples, she encourages us with truth to grow daily and motivates us to place our treasures in Heaven. If you are ready to start viewing your parenting and everyday life as Kingdom work, this book will inspire you!"
—**Leigh Ellen Chadwell**, blogger at parentingwithhumility.com

HEAVENLY MINDED

mom

A 90 DAY JOURNEY TO EMBRACE
WHAT MATTERS MOST

KATIE BENNETT

ABINGDON PRESS / NASHVILLE

HEAVENLY MINDED MOM
A 90-DAY JOURNEY TO EMBRACE WHAT MATTERS MOST

Copyright © 2018 by Abingdon Press

All rights reserved.

No part of this work may be reproduced or transmitted in any form or by any means, electronic or mechanical, including photocopying and recording, or by any information storage or retrieval system, except as may be expressly permitted by the 1976 Copyright Act or in writing from the publisher. Requests for permission can be addressed to Permissions, The United Methodist Publishing House, 2222 Rosa L. Parks Blvd., Nashville, TN, 37228 or emailed to permissions@umpublishing.org.

Library of Congress Cataloging-in-Publication Data has been requested.

ISBN 978-1-5018-4552-9

Unless otherwise indicated, all Scripture quotations are taken from the Holy Bible, New International Version®, NIV® Copyright ©1973, 1978, 1984, 2011 by Biblica, Inc.® Used by permission. All rights reserved worldwide.

Scripture quotations marked (ESV) are taken from The Holy Bible, English Standard Version. Copyright © 2001 by Crossway Bibles, a publishing ministry of Good News Publishers.

Scripture quotations marked (NLT) are taken from the *Holy Bible*, New Living Translation, copyright © 1996, 2004, 2015 by Tyndale House Foundation. Used by permission of Tyndale House Publishers Inc., Carol Stream, Illinois 60188. All rights reserved.

18 19 20 21 22 23 24 25—10 9 8 7 6 5 4 3 2 1

MANUFACTURED IN THE UNITED STATES OF AMERICA

To my husband, Mitch, who loves and elevates me as Christ does the church.

Contents

Contents

Contents

Introduction

*L*ife had always been good, but I loved it more than ever. My second beautiful baby was born. He was a wonderful, easygoing little boy. I was completely smitten with his brown eyes, calm disposition, and love for snuggling. My two-year-old daughter brimmed with curly hair, personality, and charm, and she loved her new brother very much. My full-time job was caring for my children and home while my husband worked diligently to support our family. We were a team, and we loved each other. What's more, my life had been graced with the best of friends. Everything I had dreamed for myself had come to pass, and it was all as wonderful as I had imagined and even more so. There was no disappointment to be found in any of it.

Maybe it was these idealistic circumstances, or maybe postpartum hormones played a role, but in the months that followed my son's arrival into the world I was happy—euphoric, really. I loved my life!

But as you know, life is uncertain, and so I began to be fearful. I recognized that the only direction my life could go was downhill. When would the shoe drop? I lay awake at night in fear of the calamities that could befall my husband, children, or myself, praying fervently. The constant possibility of disaster and loss felt crushing. I had everything I had ever wanted, but there was no guarantee that it would last another moment.

During this time, I also began to realize that the things I had put my hope in throughout my young life were now all behind me. I was no longer looking forward to any mysterious future phase of life. I knew what it was like to be a wife and mother, to earn and spend money, and to have a home of my own. It was all wonderful, but now *I knew*. I found myself suddenly undistracted by the exciting future possibilities that had always driven me. They were now only a glimmer in the rearview mirror.

It seemed I had come to the top of a highly anticipated, grand, and glorious mountain only to realize that even here there was a sense of emptiness. And so, as strange as it was, I began to long for hope, right there in the midst of my dream life.

And with that longing, my thoughts turned to heaven.

I entered into deep, difficult places of thought about life and death and eternity. I attempted to make sense of reality, to the point of dizziness. My finite brain struggled to grasp onto infinity, and within the mental collapse at the fringes of my understanding, the icy fingers of doubt, hopelessness, and fear gripped my heart. I began to feel panicked and detached from all I saw and heard. I cried out to God, asking to feel His presence and pleading for reassurance that the things I believed about Jesus were true. In those moments, I sensed only silence. It was an incredibly difficult time that stretched out for weeks and months. No one could help me, because no one else had any more proof than I did. They had not come back from the grave to bear witness. It had to be God. So, I stayed in the struggle and waited, wrestled, and clung to God's promises in desperation.

God emptied my life of false meaning and ill-founded hope through this season of deep thought, *but He didn't leave me empty.* He is so good.

When I had been sufficiently undone, He graciously poured faith unlike anything I had ever known into my life. He reintroduced light, hope, and certainty and then infused it with purpose and joy. It was as if the most glorious spring had come after the darkness of winter. The fruits of a reshaped perspective were vast and complete and brought with them freedom from so many fetters that had once entangled me. Like Solomon in the Book of Ecclesiastes, I saw the temporary and fleeting nature of life. It will fade away as quickly as the evening shadows and will not be remembered. I recognized the great meaninglessness and futility that is found in things that will not last. This physical world is incapable of bearing up under the weight of human hope. It cannot deliver on its promises, for it is a prisoner to decay just as we are.

In the Bible, God compares Himself to a potter. When a potter works with clay, sometimes he makes small refining adjustments to his creation. Other times, he crushes it in order to make something complete, new, better, and different. That's the best way I can describe what He did in my life through that season of undoing. He didn't give me a slightly better perspective. He gave me completely new eyes.

Today, my husband, children, friends, home, and daily life are all still there. In fact, if possible, things are better and happier now than they were those few short years ago. The difference is that I don't love my life anymore. It's not meant to last forever. I have a better hope. Jesus says it like this:

> Very truly I tell you, unless a kernel of wheat falls to the ground and dies, it remains only a single seed. But if it dies, it produces many seeds. Anyone who loves their life will lose it, while anyone who hates their life in this world will keep it for eternal life. (John 12:24-25)

In faith, we lay down foolish idols and fix our eyes on the fulfillment of the promise and the inheritance that is to come.

Treasures in Heaven

Throughout this devotional book I reference the concept of storing up treasures in heaven. If you are like me, this notion might feel awkward. Shouldn't we be loving and serving God for His sake, without a thought to what we will get out of it? Isn't seeking eternal rewards self-focused instead of God-focused?

As much as we might be inclined to reason in this way, God says quite the opposite. In fact, He inspired the writer of Hebrews 11:6 to say it like this: "without faith it is impossible to please God, because anyone who comes to him must believe that he exists and that he rewards those who earnestly seek him."

God is pleased when we believe His promise to such a degree that the unquenchable outflow is confidence that our current, earnest seeking will lead to eternal reward. What a joyful, hope-filled journey He has called us to! We have incredible promises in Christ that guarantee our inheritance as His followers. When we live like this fulfillment is actually going to happen, we assign glory to God through faith. Our obedience will be radiant in light of this hope, even as we lay down our lives and take up our cross to follow Him. God is pleased to have it this way because He loves us!

How to Read
Heavenly Minded Mom

Heavenly Minded Mom is comprised of three sequential sections. The first section is designed to open your eyes to the meaninglessness of the things we too often wrongfully align our hearts with and devote our lives to. The purpose of the first thirty days is to till up the soil of your heart and prepare it for the seeds of eternal perspective God wants to plant. It is intended to crack the thin sheet of colorful glass that is right in front of your nose (the world as you perceive it) and dethrone idols in your life so that you will be able to see past this physical existence and into eternity.

The second section of *Heavenly Minded Mom* will further cultivate your eternal perspective by demonstrating how to think and interpret life with a mind and heart set on heaven.

The third and final section of the book is about the things that will endure. It is intended to pour meaning back into the stuff of your life. The tasks, pursuits, and endeavors that were stripped of meaning at the onset of this book will be reenlivened with a different, deepened, Christ-centered sense of possibility and lasting meaning. Together, we will examine the things that will endure—faith, hope, love—and look at how we can store up treasures in heaven during our brief lives on this earth.

As tempting as it might sound from these descriptions to skip ahead to the third section, I want to encourage you to be diligent and patient. Just as the bounty of any harvest is a direct result of the effort and time spent preparing the soil and nurturing the crop, so it is with the fruit of changed perspective. The power is in the process.

My desire is to help you understand the implications of God's Word in your life and to open your eyes to eternal truth. However, my ultimate hope is that you would experience God's Word for yourself. Let me encourage you to use this devotional book as a jumping-off point for your time in God's Word and not as a replacement for it. The Scripture references at the bottom of each day's reading are an invitation for you to do just that. These verses directly correspond with the italicized words found throughout the entry with Scriptures for additional reference listed last. They provide important support, context, and opportunity for study to each devotion. Scripture references are listed in the order of their appearance as italicized phrases within the devotion. If one of these verses stirs you, I would encourage you to read the passages before and after it and to spend time carefully praying and meditating on what you have read.

Because I referenced many verses from the Book of Ecclesiastes throughout *Heavenly Minded Mom*, I have included a simple framework for understanding the Book of Ecclesiastes as an appendix to this devotional. I hope it will become one of your favorite books to read.

God's Word is living and active. It is sharper than a double-edged sword that divides even soul and spirit (Hebrews 4:12). It does not return empty, but it will accomplish what God desires (Isaiah 55:11). Exposing and submitting ourselves to this divinely inspired and empowered revelation is the ultimate avenue for a new perspective and changed life. Let us not neglect this profound gift!

As you work your way through *Heavenly Minded Mom*, you will notice a handful of themes and Scriptures that rise to the surface repeatedly in a variety of contexts. Don't be surprised by this repetition; it is intentional. I believe that the morphing of one's perspective takes time. It will require multiple opportunities to reflect along with diligent study, deep meditation (the pondering of God's Word in one's heart and mind), and real application. This devotional is not a series of disjointed thoughts but rather a journey. It is what I like to think of as "perspective therapy." My hope is that by journey's end, you not only will gain understanding of the many key passages of Scripture anchoring the message of this devotional but also will come to hold them dearly in sweet familiarity, as I do.

Day by day, you will dive down deep into this new way of seeing and then come up for air as you spend the next twenty-four hours processing and applying what you've read. There is a cyclical nature to reading and thinking. In the same way, verses, themes, and concepts will be called back in turn. Over the course of ninety days, the imminent reality of eternity will be gently massaged into your soul, and if you allow God to work in your life, your eyes will be opened to its profound earthly implications.

I have also created a collection of supplemental resources to encourage you on this journey, along with an e-mail list designed to nurture perspective in your life. Come join in! I would love to get to know you more. Find it all at www.embracingasimplerlife.com/heavenlymindedmom.

Heavenly Minded Mom in a Group Setting

Some of my favorite group discussions have been centered around devotional books. There's something uniquely gentle and nurturing about the devotion format for considering, personalizing, and applying God's truth, and there's also something indescribably sweet and intimate about coming together with other women to share the deep things God is stirring in our hearts. One member's revelation will edify the whole body of believers, and one member's pain belongs to everyone. When we encourage one another, share burdens, pray together, and apprehend God in a community, we are fulfilling God's grand design for His church.

If you would like to use this devotional to facilitate a mother's group or simply go through it with a friend, I suggest working through a set number of daily devotions individually at home throughout the week, reading the additional Scriptures listed, and making notes in the margins or in a separate journal. When you come together, simply share your personal reflections throughout the week. Use the daily questions to prompt specific discussion.

When done seven days a week, *Heavenly Minded Mom* will take approximately thirteen weeks to complete. If, for the purposes of your group, you need to fit it into a shorter time span, this devotional has been designed so you can use the first ten devotions from each of its three sections for a balanced overview of content. This will result in either a thirty-day study or a six-week study if done at the pace of five devotions per week.

A Journey Worth Taking

*I*n ninety different ways, allow me to stand at the street corner of your life and cry out the message I believe God has entrusted to me. As Isaiah wrote,

> A voice says, "Cry out."
>> And I said, "What shall I cry?"
> "All people are like grass,
>> and all their faithfulness is like the flowers of the field.
> The grass withers and the flowers fall,
>> because the breath of the Lord blows on them.
>> Surely the people are grass.
> The grass withers and the flowers fall,
>> but the word of our God endures forever."
>> (Isaiah 40:6-8)

Your life is short, and it does not hold the significance you think it does. The truth is *it holds far more.* Allow me to plead with you in so many ways to lay down your life, take up your cross, and follow Jesus more completely than ever before.

This is a journey worth taking, and I believe it will change your life. However, I must also give you fair warning: this journey is not for the faint of heart.

This is my prayer for you as you embark on this ninety-day journey.

- I pray that you would glorify God through complete surrender of your life to Him.
- I pray that you would experience the enduring peace that comes from total faith and trust.
- I pray that you would find real—eternal—meaning and fulfillment in your life.
- I pray that you would store up increased rewards in heaven as you learn to invest yourself where it matters most.

Are you ready? Let's begin!

Section One

Tilling Up the Soil

An Assault on the Idols of Your Heart

"Meaningless! Meaningless!"
says the Teacher.
"Utterly meaningless!
Everything is meaningless."
—Ecclesiastes 1:2

In Everything, There Is Futility

For the creation was subjected to frustration, not by its own choice, but by the will of the one who subjected it, in hope that the creation itself will be liberated from its bondage to decay and brought into the freedom and glory of the children of God.

—Romans 8:20-21

*I*n everything that is done in this world, there is great futility. Mothers know this well. The laundry, the dishes, the cleaning—all of these things are constantly undoing themselves. We feed our families, but they will be hungry again. We fix a problem, but our solution creates another problem. Things naturally move from organization to chaos, and we must work diligently and persistently to keep it at bay. Each day's tasks will reoccur, and in all this work there is great frustration.

Even in our childbearing there is grievance and struggle: the unpredictability of conception, the pain of pregnancy and labor, and the tear-soaked path we walk by bringing little hearts who are bent toward sin into a dark and dangerous world.

All of this futility and strife was set into motion in one fateful moment. Because of the sin of Adam and Eve, "creation was subjected to frustration" (Romans 8:20). This curse blanketed creation, and we feel it every day. As men strive to provide, they are faced with toil, thorns, and ultimately death. As women seek to be wives and mothers, we are met with pain and subjection. *Each of us is destined to return to the dust from which we came.* Our situation is not good, but God's mercy is evident even here. You see, creation was frustrated so that it might "be liberated from its bondage to decay and brought into the freedom and glory of the children of God" (8:21).

If we did not lack, how could we long for restoration and new life? If the world were whole, how could we hope in Christ? No, *we cannot hope for what we already have.* And so, we wait eagerly for "our adoption to sonship, the redemption of our bodies" (8:23).

Futility leads us to blessed disillusionment with the world so that we might see God as He is in contrast and put our hope in Him: "And hope does not put us to shame, because God's love has been poured out into our hearts through the Holy Spirit, who has been given to us" (5:5).

Embrace God's Word

For further insight, read Genesis 3:14-19 and Romans 8:18-30.

Journal Your Thoughts

What stood out to you from today's reading?

How do you see frustration and futility manifesting themselves in your own life?

God's Priorities for You

But just as he who called you is holy, so be holy in all you do; for it is written: "Be holy, because I am holy."

—1 Peter 1:15-16

*W*hat are God's priorities for you? Have you ever thought about that? Are His goals for you characterized by wealth, comfort, and ease? Is His chief hope that you would have a smooth existence on this earth? Is that the driving aim behind His work in your life?

No, of course not! God sees a far greater picture than this. He knows that your life is brief and fleeting. He knows that it will pass away in a flicker of time, and *you will reign with Him in eternity forever.* His priorities for you are not summed up by a sugar-coated, trial-free existence. Rather, He longs for you to become like Christ. He loves you, and He knows that this is far better for you.

Through very intentional work, God lovingly molds us according to His priorities. From His lofty vantage point, He sees clearly what is needed in our lives, and thus He leads us toward a place of greater maturity, depth, surrender, and dependence as we allow Him. These are the things that hold lasting value. This value utterly eclipses any and all momentary gain we might think we prefer in the present moment.

Because we cannot fully understand the scope of what God is doing in our lives or in the world—in this span of time or throughout eternity—we must trust Him. Rather than consuming our prayer lives with nothing more than requests for safety, blessing, material possessions, and success, may we also learn what it means to pray kingdom-minded prayers. May we align ourselves with the heart of God and choose to see the bigger picture that He sees.

God's priorities for our lives are deeply spiritual and eternal. Let's stop holding tightly to the things that God does not hold tightly to, and let's stop running after the things that God does not run after. *Let's be holy as He is holy. Let's strive to be perfect as He is perfect. Let's be spiritually minded as He is spiritually minded, and let's be wise as He is wise.*

Embrace God's Word

For further insight, read 2 Timothy 2:11; Matthew 5:48; Corinthians 2:10-16; and Ephesians 5:15-17.

Journal Your Thoughts

What are God's priorities for your life?

How can you join Him in the work He wants to do in you?

The Idol of Results

And I saw that all toil and all achievement spring from one person's envy of another. This too is meaningless, a chasing after the wind.

—Ecclesiastes 4:4

*T*here are many beautiful, precious outcomes of motherhood: the friendship that children add to one's life, the honor they bring, and the joy of watching them follow the Lord and do what is right. When everyone is in a sweet frame of mind and everything is going according to plan, motherhood is very fulfilling. This is the ideal I looked forward to as I awaited the arrival of my first child.

However, I quickly learned that results are slow to come by in parenting. I watched as my children, one by one, grew out of their seemingly innocent baby stages and began grappling with a startlingly rebellious nature. I learned firsthand that, try as I might, I was not in control of their hearts. In these, and in so many other ways, we weren't "there" yet—in sleep training, potty training, independence, self-discipline, character, commitment to Christ, and so on. All of these were an increasing source of frustration and failure in my life. And thus God began to open my eyes to see that I was living for successes and results rather than embracing the journey with all its struggles.

We do this often in many different ways, and not just with regard to our children. We live for achievement. We strain for the next thing: to get the pay raise at work, to grow our family, to move into that dream house, to put the diaper years behind us, to survive the sports-practice years, to successfully launch our children into the world, to reach retirement. We strain ahead, finding hope in end results and great angst in the difficulties of the process.

But that hope of "arriving"? It's a false hope. *And all those results do not hold any more meaning than does the journey to get there.* In fact, if we fixate on results, we run the risk of missing our actual lives.

Over time, God helped me slowly shift my focus away from my vain need for results. I've learned instead to set my gaze on the simple task of obeying Him right where I am—right where He has placed me. Today that means cleaning scrambled eggs off of a wooden floor, patiently disciplining and training my children, and being faithful to show up and point little hearts back to Jesus. It means thriving on the presence of God in my life, *learning contentment,* and striving to take each moment as a holy opportunity. As we learn to live the journey and trust God with the results, we gain joy, peace, and the truly *abundant life.*

Embrace God's Word

For further insight, read 1 Timothy 6:6; John 10:10; and Ecclesiastes 6:9.

Journal Your Thoughts

Reflecting on your life, do you find yourself living for results (and finding angst in the journey), or do you embrace the struggle and live in joy?

Is there a specific process in your life that God is leading you to more fully embrace?

The Idol of Seeking Possessions

*Then he said to them, "Watch out! Be on your guard against all
kinds of greed; life does not consist in an abundance of possessions."*
—Luke 12:15

Let's contrast two lives. One woman lives in a gorgeous, landscaped, well-furnished home in a beautiful neighborhood. She shops to fulfill her desires for new clothing, decor, and gadgetry, and she drives the new car of her choosing. All these things take up quite a bit of her time and attention: dreaming, planning, shopping, and managing. She is a Christian, but she has a hard time feeling content because she often sees or hears about new things she would like to have. Her life is, in large part, consumed by her possessions, just like those of her neighbors. Materialism is her culture, but it is demanding. There's always something new to want.

A second woman finds herself in a rural village in a developing country. She lives in a cinder block home with no glass in the windows, a dirt courtyard, and walls adorned with only a few sparse and tattered decorations. She keeps her living space neat, and she is grateful for it. She too is a Christian, and each day she faithfully works hard to provide for her family's most basic needs. She does not put her hope in possessions, nor does she spend much time dwelling on them at all because they are few yet adequate. Rather she puts her hope in heaven and trusts God for future reward.

The world leads us to believe that we need what the first woman has to be content and happy in life. Even Solomon explored this possibility in the Book of Ecclesiastes. He longed to find meaning in life, so he did an experiment. Solomon was a very wealthy king with almost unlimited resources at his disposal, so he decided to deny himself nothing. *He did not restrain himself from any joy, and yet all the while he remained clear eyed so he could evaluate all these things.*

Do you know what the wisest and most wealthy man on the earth discovered through this ultimate experiment? *There was nothing really worthwhile in any of it.* He saw that the pursuit of possessions and earthly pleasures was meaningless, *like chasing after the wind.* Because in the end we will all die, and all these things will vanish and cease to matter.

Both women I described above have the opportunity to follow God wholeheartedly and store up treasures in heaven. The wealthy woman is not disqualified from this pursuit, but she certainly has no advantage over the woman in humble circumstances. Neither does poverty make the second woman more holy than the first, but perhaps she has fewer obstacles to overcome in her act of surrender. The sacred task of both women is *to put their hope in God, to be generous, and to do good. That is how "they may take hold of the life that is truly life"* (1 Timothy 6:19).

Today, we must remember that possessions cannot give life meaning and that eternal purpose is found at the foot of the cross.

Embrace God's Word

For further insight, read Ecclesiastes 1:12-15; Ecclesiastes 2:1-11; and 1 Timothy 6:17-19.

Journal Your Thoughts

Which woman do you identify with most and why?

What is God calling you to do about it?

The Idol of Sin

Those who belong to Christ Jesus have crucified the flesh with its passions and desires.

—Galatians 5:24

*H*ave you ever thought about the futility and utter foolishness of sin? It is easy to downplay this truth and, as a result, allow ourselves to keep things in our lives that we should not. We believe that God will forgive us, so we are not motivated to nail our personal unforgiveness, gossip, wayward daydreams, idleness, addictions, or self-serving ways to the cross. We do not fear God, so we do not abandon sin. We keep the things we like, despite the fact that they are at odds with God's holiness.

However, the choice to sin is not only futile but also tragic. It assumes that "the now" has value over eternity. It assumes that our appetite today is more important than God's loving desire for our life. It shows our blindness to the bigger picture. The fruit borne by sin is death. When we sin knowingly and willfully, we become partners with darkness. We give it root in our lives and effectively *disassociate ourselves with those who belong to Christ*. This is why we must ruthlessly cut it out of our lives at all costs: "For as in Adam all die, so in Christ all will be made alive" (1 Corinthians 15:22). Through confessing our sins to God and acknowledging our brokenness before Him, He takes the penalty on our behalf.

When we raise our gaze to heaven and allow its light to shine into those places, the meaninglessness and calamity of these pet sins will be illuminated. We will cut away the vines that tangle up and around our feet and legs and throw them off with abandon. In this way, we are freed up to run the race God has called us to, *with heaven as the finish line and a crown of righteousness as the prize.* Without a backward glance, we "press on toward the goal" (Philippians 3:14).

Like an athlete, we exercise self-control and discipline our bodies for god-liness, but while an athlete pursues a perishable prize, we do it for one that is imperishable, lest we be disqualified. This is the eternity-soaked life.

Embrace God's Word

For further insight, read 1 John 2:4-6; Hebrews 12:1-2; 2 Timothy 4:6-8; and 1 Corinthians 9:24-27.

Journal Your Thoughts

What sin have you knowingly clung to?

Write a prayer to God asking for His strength to let it go, allowing His light to shine into that area of your life.

The Idol of Emotion

What I mean, brothers and sisters, is that the time is short. From now on those who have wives should live as if they do not; those who mourn, as if they did not; those who are happy, as if they were not; those who buy something, as if it were not theirs to keep; those who use the things of the world, as if not engrossed in them. For this world in its present form is passing away.

—1 Corinthians 7:29-31

*H*ow often we fail to understand the urgency of the mission—the urgency of the kingdom of God and its relevance to this day in which we live. This kingdom is fast approaching, like an army marching on the horizon.

Meanwhile, too many of us are caught up in our own earthly romance. Or we are left wallowing in sorrow in the aftermath of loss, disillusionment, and disappointment. Perhaps our excitement over that business opportunity or our interesting upcoming plans distract us. Many of us dig our hands deeply into the dealings of the world, and then become completely wrapped up in those things.

This leads us to spend our days planning date nights, or nurturing our identity as a suffering soul, or anticipating our next fun-filled girls' weekend. In these three diverse ways, we run the risk of making our feelings king in our lives. None of these things must be allowed to disengage us from the urgent work that God wants to accomplish through us.

Here's the truth: *the time is short!* We must not allow ourselves to be sidelined by the temporary. This is not just for our own benefit and future reward, but for the sake of others—for the sake of the kingdom of God!

The world in its present form is passing away, and yet so many Christians are numbed to this truth. As a result, we are unmotivated to get over ourselves and press on with heavenly focus. And yet, this is what we must do. The cost of distraction is high.

God is glorified in the midst of our emotions. After all, He created them! But may we always be ready to turn our face toward His glory, take up our cross, and follow Him every day and in every way. May we always be willing to submit those emotions to His enduring truths.

In it all, this is our chief concern: to *love the Lord our God with all our heart, all our soul, all our strength, and all our mind* and to "love each other deeply, because love covers over a multitude of sins" (1 Peter 4:8).

Embrace God's Word

For further insight, read Matthew 16:24; Luke 10:27; 1 Peter 4:7-8; and Matthew 24:36-44.

Journal Your Thoughts

Do you find yourself distracted by your emotions in this world, whether romance or grief or happiness? How?

What is one way that you can practically disentangle yourself from things that distract you in order to live a more urgent, heavenly minded, and kingdom-focused life?

The Idol of Busyness

He says, "Be still, and know that I am God;
I will be exalted among the nations,
I will be exalted in the earth."

—Psalm 46:10

*W*e do not live in a "still" world. There are thousands of moving pieces at any given moment in our lives, many of them vying for our time and attention: the good causes, the bad habits, the basic needs, the relationships, the entertainment, the hobbies, the work, the technology, the events, the books, the chores, the shopping, and more. We buzz around from task to task in constant thought and motion.

Busyness is not always bad. In fact, in the Bible, Paul instructed older women to teach younger women "to be busy at home" (Titus 2:5). In a culture in which most work was centered around the home, this meant busily loving one's family, busily providing for needs, and even being productive within the marketplace.

However, in our present day and time, television, computers, smartphones, instant notifications, and e-mail have elevated our opportunity for busyness. These inventions muddle up natural, God-ordained rhythms for work and rest, for busyness and stillness. From the time we wake to the time we settle into sleep, we mostly do not stop. We fill the gaps in our calendars with activities, just as we fill the gaps in our days with mindless diversions. For many of us, we have strayed from the art of stillness. Sadly, we have gotten lost in the futility of activity, and we miss *the one thing that is needed.* Instead of sitting at the feet of Jesus, we run on a hamster wheel of our own invention. This too is meaningless.

However, when we quiet our spirit and focus our heart on God, simply knowing that *He is*, it is in this stillness that we open ourselves up to the eternal. In the stillness, we find rest for our weary souls and connect with our Heavenly Father in sweet relationship. In the stillness, *God speaks to us by His Spirit and His Word*. He guides us and reveals truth as we provide space for Him to do so.

May we not run through our days distracted, with our heads down and eyes glued to the ground at our feet; may we look up and gaze upon our glorious Savior! Then, with a clear view, will we move forward in faith and grace. Then will *we hear a voice behind us saying, "This is the way; walk in it"* (Isaiah 30:21).

Let's take time this week to *wait on the Lord and renew our strength*. Let's be still, and let's do it on purpose.

Embrace God's Word

For further insight, read John 14:25-27; Isaiah 40:30-31; Psalm 23:1-6; and Luke 10:38-42.

Journal Your Thoughts

Right now, quiet your heart before the Lord. As you are ready, look up and read the Scripture references and surrounding verses.

What is God saying to you through His Spirit and His Word?

Have you allowed the idol of busyness to take priority in your life at the expense of the things that matter most?

The Idol of a Pain-Free Life

"The LORD gave and the LORD has taken away;
may the name of the LORD be praised."

—Job 1:21b

*D*o you ever struggle with fear, perhaps lying awake at night as I have imagining different kinds of disasters that could befall your family? Or perhaps your greatest fear has become reality, and you question how you could ever know true peace and trust again. The temptation to fear in this world is real. Even while I had only good gifts in my life, I was bent out of shape by apprehension. The potential for suffering and loss was overwhelming. Stories of tragedy deeply disturbed me. I especially feared losing my husband or children.

But the truth is, we have no guarantee of a pain-free life, nor that we will never experience loss. If our best hope is that nothing bad will happen, we have little hope indeed. Death is our imminent reality.

Yet we serve a big, good, sovereign, and wise God. He does not always protect us from suffering in this life because He sees an eternal picture. He knows that trials provide us with an opportunity to be refined. Surely, *the one who has suffered is done with sin*, and it is by fire that gold is purified. *Through suffering, false hope is stripped away and replaced with real, eternal hope.* Our loving Father knows that it is only in the midst of suffering that we have the opportunity to persevere and that it is through this perseverance that we store up treasures in heaven that will last for eternity. Our suffering isn't just a curse. It's also a gift.

Just as Job did when he lost all he had (children, livestock, and health), we have the opportunity to remain faithful when we suffer loss, receiving from the Lord both the good things and bad and trusting Him to our last breath, regardless of our limited understanding. Job's yielded heart assigned glory to God not just on the earth but in the heavenly realms. Our God is worthy, holy, and mighty! *We have been crucified with Christ, and we no longer live, but Christ lives in us. The life we live in the body we live by faith in the Son of God who loved us and gave His life for us!* If we believe that, we will trustingly receive from Him the life He has apportioned to us.

It was through a realization of these eternal truths that God set me free from the fear I once knew. I still deeply want good things for my family, but I no longer believe that I "need" them or that this life is the be-all and end-all. Rather, I surrender them to Jesus, knowing that this life is exceedingly short compared to eternity, knowing that He loves them beyond comprehension, and knowing that He is trustworthy. That same freedom is for you too. Rather than try to control the uncontrollable, let us make it our mission to live each day in faithfulness, wisdom, love, and obedience to God, however that may look. Let us live a life of confident hope.

Embrace God's Word

For further insight, read 1 Peter 4:1-5; Romans 5:3-5; Job 1; and Galatians 2:20.

Journal Your Thoughts

What fears specifically do you struggle with most?

How are you reconciling your personal fears with eternal truths?

The Idol of an Easy Life

Blessed is the man who remains steadfast under trial, for when he has stood the test he will receive the crown of life, which God has promised to those who love him.

—James 1:12 ESV

*A*s a mom of little kids, I miss "easy." I remember what it was like to walk into a grocery store and quietly make decisions, unencumbered by so many impatient or chatty or excited or discontent companions. I used both hands to steer the cart out to the car and looked forward to putting my feet up once groceries for two people were safely put away at home. I remember what it was like to sit down to dinner with friends or with my husband and have an uninterrupted conversation. I remember a time when things around the house stayed where I put them and when I only cleaned up messes I chose to create.

However, when children came in through the front door of my life, ease and control sneaked out the back. Life isn't as easy as it once was, and I notice that. It gives me pause. Moms often remark that life will get easier again soon, and I believe them. But I also wonder, what value does an easy life hold eternally? Is this a worthy hope for my life in the future as I watch, or even wait (in some instances), for my kids to grow up?

Much of our society and culture center on this very value, the value of pursing and ensuring an easy life. This is what we are trained and conditioned to desire and idealize. Why would we have lots of children when children require such hard work? Why would we foster or adopt when that is such a sacrifice?

But when you actually think about it, ease doesn't matter past the moment in which it's lived. In fact, every easy moment is one less opportunity to be groomed into the likeness of Christ. It's one less opportunity *to remain steadfast under trial* (and thereby store up future rewards) and one less chance to give glory to God by trusting Him in the midst of hardship.

When considered in light of eternity, rather than longing for easy, *we will instead consider it pure joy when we face trials, for we know with confidence that they will bring about good fruit in our lives.* Maturing isn't easy or painless, but it is inexplicably good. In and through the presence of these very difficulties, we have the privilege of drinking from the well of God's grace more deeply than ever before. *We learn of its sufficiency and see God's power flow through our lives completely.* We experience joy as we endure hard things with our eyes fixed on heaven, knowing that God is good, and that He is doing a good work in our lives through each hard moment.

Let's stop comparing our lives to those of others. Let's refrain from putting undue hope in the days ahead when our kids will become incrementally more independent or, on the other hand, glamorizing and glossing over the difficulties of life. Let's let the good things be good and the hard things be good too as we learn to rely on grace and lift our gaze heavenward.

Embrace God's Word

For further insight, read James 1:2-4; 2 Corinthians 12:9; and Romans 8:18-28.

Journal Your Thoughts

At what points of your life have you been discontent when things were hard?

How could you surrender the expectation of an easy life, let go of control, and joyfully live out of God's abundant grace?

The Idol of Entertainment

Finally, brothers and sisters, whatever is true, whatever is noble, whatever is right, whatever is pure, whatever is lovely, whatever is admirable—if anything is excellent or praiseworthy—think about such things.

—Philippians 4:8

*I*n this day and age, much of our lives are consumed with entertaining ourselves. Many of us spend hours every single day watching television, scrolling through social media, or playing games on our smartphones or computers. It would seem one of our central goals in life is simply to keep ourselves amused moment by moment.

Yesterday's entertainment holds little or no value today, so we must keep feeding our appetites. Night after night we sit in front of the television, all the while feeling discouraged about our lack of time to pray, to read God's Word consistently, or to spend time with our families. When we finish one television series, we move onto the next, even if that means moving on to the next best. Anything is better than nothing, so our standards dip.

Why do we invest so much of our lives into entertainment? Why do we willingly ingest things that ultimately lead our minds and hearts away from God by promoting untruth? Or maybe our chosen form of entertainment isn't necessarily unholy, but it consistently distracts us from the things that matter most. Either way, it can easily become an idol. Perhaps we crave diversion from strained relationships or unmet expectations. Perhaps we crave rest. Perhaps picking up our smartphone is simply our default action, so we give it no further thought.

However, at the end of a life, all those thousands upon thousands of hours we devoted to our own entertainment will be meaningless and gone. It is wonderful to enjoy the good gifts God has given us, but so often we settle for a sorry second to all that He is offering us. We fail to soak our minds *in that which is true, noble, right, pure, lovely, admirable, excellent, and praiseworthy.* We fail to raise our eyes and consider the eternal implications of how we spend our time today.

If only we would commit to be fully present and available in relationships, even when they are hard. If only we would allow ourselves the space to be alone with our thoughts rather than filling the silence. If only we would experience real rest (it's called sleep) rather than the half-rest provided by digital diversions.

A few years ago, I decided to pursue blogging and writing. Because I had two young children at home with another one on the way, I had to make some hard decisions about how I would find the time to write. Early on, I chose to give up my daily habit of watching television. I am amazed at how much this one small change opened up my soul to God and added abundance to my life! In addition to finding time to work at home, I sleep more, rest better, hear God more clearly, think more deeply, and spend more quality time with my family.

Reexamine the role of entertainment in your life, and do not withhold this thing from God if He is calling you to make a change in how you spend your life.

Embrace God's Word

For further insight, read Ecclesiastes 1:1-11; Romans 12:1-2; and 1 John 2:15-17.

Journal Your Thoughts

How does entertainment in your life add glory to God? How does it hold enduring value for you?

If you feel that it has no value to you, what challenge could you give yourself to abstain from entertainment and to focus more on God?

The Idol of Chasing Dreams

*But godliness with contentment is great gain, for we brought
nothing into the world, and we cannot take anything out of the
world.*

—1 Timothy 6:6-7 ESV

*T*hose big dreams we are cherishing and pursuing? Chasing them is like
chasing after the wind.

Our career? Our striving for fame or success? Our ceaseless pursuit
of that thing we want? These aspirations grab our hearts and consume our
lives. We devote our time, effort, and attention to their realization and years
of our lives to achieving our dream. Perhaps we work extra hours and lose
sleep. Perhaps we become stressed and grumpy, and it shows in how we treat
others. Or maybe we feel dejected because we do not have a dream or know
our dream. As this dream narrative plays out in our lives, we run the risk of
focusing on the wrong thing entirely.

My husband and I both work to generate an income from home through
self-employment endeavors. We work hard not only to make ends meet but
also to have the financial freedom in our lives. It's easy to burn the candle at
both ends in an attempt to generate money and success. But the thing I've
noticed is this: more money and more success do not actually satisfy the
soul. Rather, true satisfaction is found in the discipline of contentment no
matter the circumstances.

What is your biggest and best dream? Imagine dedicating your life to it.
Imagine seeing it come true as a result of your life's devotion!

Now, imagine coming to the end of your time on this earth: the heavens
will disappear with a roar and the earth and everything done in it will be laid

bare. There you will stand before the throne of God. Will you be glad for the way you invested your time, talents, and resources? Will that dream matter? If it was centered on something that holds eternal value (seeing the gospel advanced, investing in new believers who grow in maturity, and so on) then, yes! If your dream was more about getting ahead or enjoying yourself, then no, probably not. Everything you've pursued for your own acclaim and satisfaction will be gone. In fact, in God's upside-down economy, "many who are first will be last, and many who are last will be first" (Matthew 19:30).

Although our worldly dreams may well be void of inherent lasting value, neither are they evil. In fact, when these same dreams are wholeheartedly surrendered to the God who created us to dream, they can become beautiful offerings to Him. When we unclench our fists and entrust our dreams to God, we have the privilege of moving in His grace, according to His leading. This is where joy and abundant life reside!

So, do this now. Open your hands, literally, and pray. Recognize the emptiness or true value within your dreams and give them to the God who loves you.

Embrace God's Word

For further insight, read Ecclesiastes 5:15-16 and Revelation 6:14.

Journal Your Thoughts

How do your ambitions and pursuits distract you from living an eternally significant life?

How do your dreams line up with eternal values?

The Idol of Motherhood

No one remembers the former generations,
and even those yet to come
will not be remembered
by those who follow them.

—Ecclesiastes 1:11

*W*hat is the meaning of things forgotten?

Throughout history there have been many mothers who have lived and died. These women cherished, disciplined, and cared for their children well. They made sacrifices and worked diligently, and as a result, these children grew and went out into the world. They were successful and had families of their own. These children had children, and the older generations, one by one, passed away. For a time, these great mothers were remembered, but slowly that memory faded away as those who knew them also died. Eventually, all record of countless mothers throughout history and across the face of the earth faded from anyone's knowledge. Not only was their existence ultimately forgotten but also that of their children, grandchildren, and so on.

Even the most distant descendent will someday be gone. The world and all it holds will pass away. At the end of time, none will be left on this earth who hold any knowledge of the things of the world. All knowledge will pass away, along with every monument and history book.

The lasting meaning in our mothering will not be the straight As our children earned nor their starting position on the soccer team. It will not be the way others admired or complimented us. It will not be the stylish outfits our children wore, the fun activities we planned, or the good manners we insisted they practice. All of this will be completely forgotten under the sun. Those who were impressed will die and know no more.

However, what *will* matter eternally is the way we lay down our life each and every day to follow Jesus. Lasting meaning will be found the way we trust God and obey Him wholeheartedly. It will be found in the way we faithfully commit our mothering task to Him and carry it out for His glory. In this way, our efforts become holy and eternal. When done for God's glory and pleasure, every meaningless thing becomes significant in realms beyond that which we can see.

It is the moment-by-moment, simple acknowledgement and surrender to God in our hearts that shift our gaze to heaven and infuse lasting meaning into this life under the sun.

Embrace God's Word

For further insight, read Ecclesiastes 2:14-16; 1 John 2:17; 1 Corinthians 7:29-31; and Romans 12:1.

Journal Your Thoughts

Imagine a time in the future when you will be forgotten on the earth, like so many before you. What is your reaction to that thought?

How does this eternal paradigm change your perspective of motherhood?

The Idol of Human Wisdom

As the heavens are higher than the earth,
so are my ways higher than your ways
and my thoughts than your thoughts.

—Isaiah 55:9

*I*t is easy to take a convenient view of God rather than allow His Word to speak for itself. It is tempting to squeeze Scripture to fit in with our preconceived notions and determinations about who He is. By glossing over some passages, taking others out of context, and setting others aside completely as anomalies, we do the dangerous work of interpreting God's Word according to our understanding. We rely on faulty wisdom and "force" God to fit who we think He should be in our own minds. We see Him as nothing more than a bigger and better version of ourselves. I know this because I've been guilty of it myself at various times and in different, subtle ways.

But here's the thing about God: He is entirely separate from us. He isn't contrived or created; He just *is*. The very name with which He described himself to the people He created in the world and reality He imagined is "I AM" (Exodus 3:14). What a mysterious and wonderful God we serve! He is completely holy, completely good, and completely right. He is more than we could ever imagine or know. *His ways are higher than our ways, and His thoughts are higher than our thoughts.* He is calling us to know and receive and love and trust Him on His terms, not ours. In fact, *it is in this very knowing that the essence of our eternal life is found.* This eternal life starts now, not later when we die. It is unleashed in our lives when we lay down our arguments, stubborn sin, and reservations, and recognize that God *is who He is* and seek to know Him as such.

This is why we must read and interpret the Bible in context of itself, with an openhanded, humble, and honest heart. We must trustingly live in the tension of things we don't understand rather than explain them away. We must revere God and recognize His great patience and kindness toward us, that He would allow us to be so prideful and yet still draw and beckon us deeper into truth. We must surrender our thoughts and ways and submit them to His complete and enduring truth.

Embrace God's Word

For further insight, read John 17:3; Exodus 3:13-14; and 2 Timothy 3:16-17.

Journal Your Thoughts

How are you at letting God be God?

In what ways do you find it easy or difficult to trust Him completely, especially when you don't understand all that you are reading in Scripture?

The Idol of More

Better one handful with tranquility
than two handfuls with toil
and chasing after the wind.

—Ecclesiastes 4:6

*W*hen we fail to see past the facade of the world in front of us, our lives will be characterized by folly. We will be too easily consumed with the accumulation of more, bigger, and better. The pitiable pursuit of material possessions and pleasure will pull us in like an ocean current, and we will unintentionally devote our lives to acquiring things that could never replace the peace, hope, and joy of contentment in Christ.

"More" focused living leads us to encumber ourselves with debt, which in turn prevents us from giving generously to the needs of others. We work extra jobs to afford that mortgage and those upgrades on that new vehicle. We feel we must have two handfuls because they look oh-so appealing, so we toil and chase the wind to have them.

"More" focused living leads us to consume our minds with what we want and how we are going to get it. We devote hours upon hours to dreaming and shopping, either browsing in stores or online. If we're not careful, this searching and wanting shoulders out the eternal and replaces it with things that will perish, spoil, and fade.

What do we really gain from all our striving? In reality, nothing but dust and disappointment. The moment of excitement in which we get what we want is as fleeting as the wind. That new car will soon be stained and scratched; that new furniture will be nicked; that new outfit will cease to delight us.

Let us learn what it means to find tranquility in what we have and to live well within our means. This will enable us to give lavishly to God's kingdom work as He leads. May we release our wish lists to God. When we allow Him to be the guardian of our desires, He will decide whether to lovingly give them back to us or to help us see their relative unimportance and guide us down a better, simpler, and more abundant path.

Embrace God's Word

For further insight, read Hebrews 13:5; 1 Timothy 6:6-11; and Proverbs 15:16.

Journal Your Thoughts

In what areas of your life are you naturally "more" focused?

How could you invite the principle in Ecclesiastes 4:6 into these areas?

The Idol of People-Pleasing

Am I now trying to win the approval of human beings, or of
God? Or am I trying to please people? If I were still trying to
please people, I would not be a servant of Christ.
—Galatians 1:10

*A*controlling desire for the approval of others is like a heavy weight tied
onto our legs. People-pleasing is not a good thing because it leads us to feel
we must have the approval of others to be okay. It is ultimately rooted in
insecurity and in the subtle doubt of the truth of what God says about us.
This perceived need will hamstring our effort to run the race to which God
is calling us. *If we are seeking the approval of mankind, we cannot also serve*
Christ. Additionally, our motivation for this type of living is not actually
about loving those we are seeking to please. Rather, it is about gaining something for ourselves in the form of merit, false worth, or a sense of control.

This is done not so that the kingdom of God may move forward, but so
that we may feel okay.

When I was a teen, the social dynamic of high school felt all important
to me. I went through school with 150 peers in a small town. We all knew
one another on some level. At the time, I felt I *needed* teachers and classmates
to have a positive perception of me, and I was not going to say or do anything to jeopardize that. If some dissatisfaction was expressed toward me, it
was crushing. I couldn't see past this fishbowl reality until I graduated and
moved on. It was freeing! Now, high school is nothing more than a dim and
distant memory. What those individuals thought or think of me does not
define me in any way, and I now see that it never did. I soon recognized that
there is a much bigger world at hand.

In the same way that high school turned out to be far less important than I thought at the time, the people and opinions surrounding you and me now will very soon fade away into oblivion. Attaining the approval of those around us doesn't matter in the way we sometimes think it does. In fact, it is eternally tragic when we live out the one life we've been given trying to please people rather than trying to please Christ.

Today I'm challenging you to release your need for approval from parents, neighbors, coworkers, friends, and even those in authority. May we love them and work for their good for the sake of Christ, not because we somehow need them to esteem us. *Let us throw off those weights, fix our eyes on Christ alone, and* "run with perseverance the race marked out for us" (Hebrews 12:1).

Embrace God's Word

For further insight, read Hebrews 12:1-2; Proverbs 29:25; and 1 Corinthians 10:31-33.

Journal Your Thoughts

Is there an area of your life where God is calling you to lay down your need for approval in order to fully and completely follow Him?

This may even look like being a disappointment to an individual. How will you know you're still loving those you're disappointing?

The Idol of Personal Projects

Everyone comes naked from their mother's womb,
and as everyone comes, so they depart.
They take nothing from their toil
that they can carry in their hands.

—Ecclesiastes 5:15

I slowly scrape and peel at the edges of the 1980s striped-and-floral wallpaper adorning the walls in the bathroom of our new home. As I do, I think about the man who built this house several decades ago. I know a bit of his story. He was bachelor, living alone. He bought this property in the country and custom-designed a home just the way he wanted it. This included luxuries such as a Jacuzzi tub surrounded by beautiful rock finishes and large windows overlooking a lake; skylights throughout; and a massive, high-end fireplace, just to name a few. He lived here for many years, and then, as we all will, he died. Although the house changed hands a few times since then, now it is ours. And by this point in time, the styles are solidly outdated, and it needs plenty of work.

As my husband and I busy ourselves reimagining and changing this space, I wonder about him. I think about how special this home must have been to him and how he must have enjoyed it. I imagine him selecting this obviously original wallpaper, which was very stylish at the time and taking pleasure in how it looked when the project was completed. I consider his loss of control over his (former) home now that he is gone, and I see that this will also be true for me after I am gone. I am excited to enjoy the final product when our remodel is done, but I cannot take it with me any more than he could. My enjoyment of this house will do me no ultimate or lasting good. This too is meaningless.

For this reason, wisdom dictates that our possessions and personal projects must be secondary in our lives. They must be subordinate to *God's kingdom work*. While having a nice home can be a blessing from God and a tool used to meet the needs of our own families and others through hospitality, it can also be a foolish distraction and even an idol. May we not justify an extravagant home with the excuse of using it to "bless" others when this is not our true motive. Let's be brutally honest with ourselves before God because the time is short!

May our minds and finances and hearts not be bound up in that which is utterly temporary, but may we "use the things of this world, as if not engrossed in them. For this world in its present form is passing away" (1 Corinthians 7:31).

Embrace God's Word

For further insight, read Matthew 6:33 and Psalm 39:6.

Journal Your Thoughts

Does it make you sad to think that you will lose control of your worldly possessions after you die? If so, ask God to help you loosen your grip on them.

What personal projects are you currently pursuing? Are these projects idols in your life, or are they subordinate to God's kingdom agenda?

The Idol of Fun Experiences

Enjoy life … all the days of this meaningless life that God has
given you under the sun—all your meaningless days. For this is
your lot in life and in your toilsome labor under the sun.
—Ecclesiastes 9:9

I've always liked the concept of a bucket list. This is a list of things a person wants to do and see before he or she "kicks the bucket." Although I've never taken the time to make one for myself, it seems a whimsical and poignant thing to do. The idea of having hopes and goals and then fulfilling them is appealing.

There is nothing wrong with tasting, seeing, doing, and enjoying the things God has created according to a personal bucket list, but, nonetheless, eternity begs an entirely different way of looking at life. Consider for a moment all the people who have created and fulfilled such a list who are now dead. What did they really gain? That Disney vacation, that biking adventure, and that skydiving trip are forever over and forgotten. These things cannot be enjoyed from the grave. As Solomon surveyed the milling about of humanity under the sun, he observed that

> the living know that they will die,
>   but the dead know nothing;
> they have no further reward,
>   and even their name is forgotten.

(Ecclesiastes 9:5)

What's more, in its very nature, a bucket list is mostly self-serving. It is centered around what we want out of life. It is a collection of our random desires. These desires are not bad, but we must realize that our lives hold a greater purpose than whatever pleasures and interesting experiences we could dream up to strive for within this life.

Can you imagine the apostles scheming and planning their lives around a typical bucket list? No, they were occupied with a mission far more urgent, and they understood that the wonders yet to come would be worth every sacrifice.

We, too, have confident knowledge in the fuller picture of God's redemptive and eternal work in the world. We know that through placing our faith in Christ and surrendering our lives to God, we become *a new creation, a living stone in His altar*, and a recipient of eternal life. What a glorious hope! In this way, our lives become about Him and His kingdom, not about us and our desires at all.

Let me encourage you today to give your hopes and goals to the Lord. Allow Him to be the Keeper of these desires. Give Him your life to the last drop to do with as He pleases. He may give your bucket list right back to you (He loves to bless His children), or He may even give you something far better either in this life or in the next.

Embrace God's Word

For further insight, read 2 Corinthians 5:17 and 1 Peter 2:4-6.

Journal Your Thoughts

Do you have a bucket list you are working to fulfill? If so, take time to surrender it to God.

How could your bucket list get in the way of living an eternally significant life? How could these goals promote it?

The Idol of Financial Security

Calling his disciples to him, Jesus said, "Truly I tell you, this poor widow has put more into the treasury than all the others. They all gave out of their wealth; but she, out of her poverty, put in everything—all she had to live on."

—Mark 12:43-44

*M*y husband and I diligently save for our retirement. We have no problem making significant lifestyle sacrifices to be able to store away what we know we will appreciate later!

But what about our "eternal retirement account," so to speak? In the same way we make hard choices and do without to be able to store up wealth for later in life, we also have the opportunity to store up treasures in heaven by investing financially in God's kingdom and seeing the gospel spread as a result! We know that *He will reward our unacknowledged and cheerful sacrifice for the sake of His people.* These rewards will last forever. This is unfathomable, but we can trust what God has said.

Unfortunately, the standards of this world skew our perspectives. The cultural blinders go up, and we can't see beyond the quartz countertops, iPhones, cable television, and beach vacations that we expect. Too often we give God our leftovers, and that only after we've sufficiently padded ourselves up on every side. We must ruthlessly examine our hearts to discover our true motives: Are we foolishly valuing money and all it brings? Or are we walking in full faith with our lifestyle, ready to hand it over at any moment should God ask it of us?

Our world values financial security. It makes sense, and yes, there is sound judgment in saving for retirement and such. This is a good thing to do.

But too often we idolize our efforts. We want to be in control of the future. We think of ourselves first, and we justify the stoking of our accounts under the flag of wisdom. What if we were more passionate and concerned with being a part of what God is doing across the world and advancing His name than we are with protecting our own futures? Futures that may never come? What if we believe that God will provide for our needs as He said He would? True wisdom sees spiritual truth. True wisdom exercises faith.

Let me challenge you today to perceive and steward your worldly possessions and wealth with eternity in mind. It's not the amount of money that matters. *Rather, it's the amount of sacrifice.* May God be glorified in our giving!

Embrace God's Word

For further insight, read Matthew 6:3-4; 2 Corinthians 9:6-7; Luke 16:13; and Malachi 3:10.

Journal Your Thoughts

How does your giving and use of resources reflect a heart that is set on things above or a heart that is bound up in the world?

How have you exercised faith through sacrificial giving in the past? How have you seen God work through your sacrifice?

The Idol of Achievement

What do people get for all the toil and anxious striving with which they labor under the sun? All their days their work is grief and pain; even at night their minds do not rest. This too is meaningless.

—Ecclesiastes 2:22-23

*A*t the end of time, what will become of all our earthly achievements? They will cease to matter. The world will vanish. Reality will be cracked open, and we will see things in a new way.

When I started my career, I was a teacher. I had lofty goals. I wanted to be inspiring to my students and achieve acclaim and good test scores. Even when I took a step back to become a stay-at-home mom when my first child was born, I aspired to use my time at home to obtain a doctorate degree and eventually become a curriculum coordinator for a large school district. I excelled in academic settings, so I felt I could stand out and be successful. I wanted to get my next degree from not just any university, but from the most impressive university available. This would have been a huge investment of years of my life.

But the fact is, those pursuits were meaningless and vain because they were rooted in the thirst for personal glory. This is maddeningly futile because it leads our hearts away from God, and it will not last. The new broadened and heightened perspective dawning in my life soon drained my heart of this self-glorifying dream. In fact, even something so simple as my work as a stay-at-home-mom was stripped of the false sense of purpose that shrouded it. The home improvement projects, the income building, the daily tasks and rewarding moments—all of it was meaningless, like chasing after the wind.

And yet, it is in this dizzying (and merciful) rifting of the world in front of our noses that God breathes new purpose and eternal significance into our toil and striving. By His grace, the things we choose to work toward, and most importantly why we do them, undergo a cosmic shift.

When we learn what it means to wholly give our lives to God, and when we lay down our vain ambitions at the foot of the cross, it is here that we will live without regrets.

In this place of surrender, God begins the sweet process of aligning our will with His own. He may give us the very same ambitions we started with, but our heart position and motivation will most likely be completely different. Or God may give us a new vision altogether. Either way, when we walk in humble obedience, when we bend our hearts to God, and when we offer to do our work unto Him, for His fame and glory, we will receive an eternal inheritance from the Lord as our reward. When we understand the spiritual equation for work, we will do it in a way that truly matters.

Embrace God's Word

For further insight, read Colossians 3:23-24; Luke 9:25; Matthew 6:33; and Ephesians 2:10.

Journal Your Thoughts

What achievements in your life seemed significant at the time, but you now realize do not ultimately matter?

What ambitions in your life, if any, is God calling you to lay down in light of eternity?

The Idol of Family

*Anyone who loves their father or mother more than me is not
worthy of me; anyone who loves their son or daughter more than
me is not worthy of me. Whoever does not take up their cross and
follow me is not worthy of me. Whoever finds their life will lose it,
and whoever loses their life for my sake will find it.*

—Matthew 10:37-39

*B*ecause we are mothers, our families can gain territory in our hearts they
were not meant to possess. If we find ourselves loving our husbands and children more than God, we have created an idol.

Jesus tells us that the first and greatest commandment given by God is
to love the Lord our God with all our heart, all our soul, and all our mind. He
says that *anyone who loves their son or daughter more than Him is not worthy of
Him.* Yet in a society where the idolization of family and children is glorified
and touted, it is grievously easy to give our love and allegiance to them and
to look to family for fulfillment. I didn't know it at the time, but this was my
daily reality just a few short years ago. I was more consumed and enamored
with my family than with my Lord.

This must not be. We must not allow ourselves to become so happily
wrapped up in our families that we miss the spiritual and eternal reality. And
so, perspective was the thing that did the difficult work of wrenching this
out of my heart. I saw that this precious family unit of mine will pass away.
This structure is not meant to be an idol or a stumbling block, and it will not
endure in its present form. God's beautiful design for family has been broken
and marred by sin: from the abandoned child, to the grief-stricken mother, to
the selfish spouse. We know that *there will be no marriage after the Resurrection*

and that our children will stand beside us on the day of judgment to give personal account for their actions and choices.

Let us invite God in to gently and painfully loosen the world-focused crust on our eyes and teach us to give our hearts to Jesus only. When we do, we will be empowered to love our families out of the overflow of God's love in us. After all, *the second greatest commandment is like the first: to love others as we love ourselves.* We must learn to love others on God's errand, with His overpowering, complete, and burning love. It is far more abundant and sacrificial than any love we could ever dream to offer on our own strength. It is this love that our families truly crave.

It is this love that will endure.

As we set our hearts on heaven, we will no longer expect or pressure our family to fill our heart's deepest needs, which they cannot do. We will instead joyfully serve and love them in obedience to Christ.

Embrace God's Word

For further insight, read Matthew 22:29-30, 34-40; Matthew 10:37; and 1 John 4:7-14.

Journal Your Thoughts

Do you struggle with idolizing your family? Take time to offer them to God.

Do you struggle with the idea that idolizing your family is truly wrong? If so, why?

The Idol of Earthly Treasures

Do not be afraid, little flock, for your Father has been pleased to
give you the kingdom. Sell your possessions and give to the poor.
Provide purses for yourselves that will not wear out, a treasure
in heaven that will never fail, where no thief comes near and no
moth destroys. For where your treasure is, there your heart will
be also.

—Luke 12:32-34

I recently heard a fictitious illustration about a man who devoted himself to the accumulation of wealth throughout his life. He was a Christian, and yet he desperately wanted to take his life's work with him to heaven when he died.

In the story, the man petitioned God for this opportunity, and God agreed to let him do this. To make the traveling easier, the man converted his wealth into gold coins. When it was all said and done, he had a bag containing two hundred pounds of gold. Then he died.

He soon found himself walking down the streets of heaven. He struggled under the weight of the bag slung over his shoulder. Two bystanders watched the scene unfold, puzzled. One turned to the other and whispered, "I wonder, why is he bringing in that bag of pavement?"

You see, the very streets in heaven are made of gold! God's economy is completely foreign to what we know. The man in this story is foolish for so many reasons. He had no understanding of worth. He completely miscalculated how to invest his life, and in doing so, he missed the point of his existence. This is far more sad than comical.

And yet too often we live our lives in the very same way, accumulating experiences, worldly possessions, and wealth with no thought to their eternal value. We put ourselves ahead of others and allow money and possessions to distract us from spiritual realities. May it not be so!

God is holy. He is a consuming fire. He has loved us with an everlasting love, and He has sacrificed His very Son to redeem our lives from the pit. The mission of the kingdom of God is urgent. Even now, the day of judgment is at hand, and on *that day, the true worth of every life's work will be revealed.*

So I ask you, what would it mean for you to deny yourself, take up your cross, and follow Jesus today? What would it mean for you to fix your eyes on heaven and run the race marked out for you with perseverance? What would it mean for you to believe God's promises and live like they are true—His promise that *He will reward every sacrifice you make on this earth for the sake of the kingdom?*

Let us not waste our lives. Life is too short and God is too good! This earth and all it holds is passing away. *God generously gives us many things for our enjoyment,* but may they never take the lead in our lives.

Embrace God's Word

For further insight, read 1 Corinthians 3:10-15; Matthew 19:28-30; and 1 Timothy 6:17.

Journal Your Thoughts

Are there earthly treasures in your life that you are overvaluing? How?

How does your life currently reflect the mission of God's kingdom?

The Idol of World Betterment

If I give all I possess to the poor and give over my body to hard-
ship that I may boast, but do not have love, I gain nothing.
— 1 Corinthians 13:3

*T*here are many people in this world who try to find meaning in the good
of humanity. These individuals adopt a line of thinking that says humans
are basically good, and that together, we can be a force for good in the world
through channeling the love within us. Through making some kind of positive impact, we will find significance and somehow attain lasting meaning.

While this humanitarian viewpoint might seem a little "off" to you, I
think even Christians can get pulled in to it on some level. I've heard it said
that the most deceptive falsehoods are those that are 90 percent true. We
know God calls us to do good and to serve others. But here's the last ten
percent: our attempts at world betterment, when done apart from Christ,
are meaningless.

Humans are not basically good; we are inherently evil. Our version of
love is ultimately self-serving. We help others because it makes us feel good
about ourselves or because we want to impress or because we are seeking to
matter. Real love is far deeper, more sacrificial, and wholly rooted in God.
In fact, *we are not ultimately capable of functioning in complete love apart from*
God, who Himself is the essence and embodiment of love. It is not something
we can draw from within ourselves, but something that must be drawn
from Him.

No matter what good we do, if it is not birthed from and carried out in
love, *we gain nothing, we have nothing, we are nothing.*

The truth is, we will die. And that person we helped? He or she will die. Any worldly advantage will vanish, along with all our self-assigned glory and sufficiency. Everyone who thought highly of us will die too, and our good deeds, if done apart from love, will not be remembered.

Therefore, let's submit ourselves to God's love, admit our depravity, and learn what it means to do good works and love others in His power.

Embrace God's Word

For further insight, read 1 John 4:7-12; 1 Corinthians 13:1-6; and Matthew 7:21-23.

Journal Your Thoughts

What surprises you today?

Where do your good deeds find their source?

The Idol of the American Dream

*Do not work for food that spoils, but for food that endures to
eternal life, which the Son of Man will give you.*

—John 6:27a

What does the American Dream look like for us as mothers? Perhaps it is
the classic picture of wealth, career success, influence, and achievement. Or
perhaps it is characterized by the white picket fence, loving husband, ador-
able children, and our recent magazine-ready family photo shoot, complete
with coordinating outfits, whimsical sun flare, candid smiles, and a flurry of
compliments on Facebook. We all see it. It's the dream, and it beckons.

So, like chasing after the wind, we consume ourselves with the pursuit
of every available modern convenience, pleasure, treasure, and picture-
perfect appearance. And each of these things will disappoint us in turn.

- How many families have fallen by the wayside as a result of men
  and women devoting themselves to worldly achievement?
- How many individuals have lost their health or completely missed
  out on the truly sweet and simple things in life in the course of
  their personal rat race?
- How many gorgeous family photos on social media are a facade for
  loneliness, brokenness, and pain?
- How many once optimistic youths have ended up disillusioned
  and discouraged?

Many, many, many, and many. The truth is, the American Dream is
hollow. Yes, opportunity is a gift and we should be grateful! But still, its

pursuit doesn't matter in an eternal way. This dream leads us to believe that the answer to our life is an ideal, but this ideal will not satisfy. It will not fortify us for difficult days. It will not endure past the moment in which it is enjoyed. Too often as Christians we attempt to make biblical principles fit into the America Dream lifestyle. Instead, we are called to be set apart. We are called to allow the Bible and its truth to shape our vision and purpose in life.

When we seek first the kingdom of God and His righteousness, everything that we need will be added to us, and so much more. When we lay aside the American Dream and instead take up contentment, servanthood, and sacrifice, we will reap the fruit of righteousness and joy. God may give us that magazine-cover family, that quaint home, and those walls filled with beautiful photos and memories. He may give us wealth and influence and prosperity, but it will be for His purposes and in His time. Or He may not. We do know that whatever He gives us will come in addition to an abiding peace that will not shift with the tide of income and circumstance.

Let us not pursue the American Dream at the expense of the kingdom of God.

Embrace God's Word

For further insight, read Matthew 6:19-34; Colossians 3:12-17; and 1 John 2:15-17.

Journal Your Thoughts

Are you busying yourself pursuing the American Dream? How could you turn your heart to more eternal things?

Where is the good in the American Dream? Where does it fall short?

The Idol of Wants

Don't store up treasures here on earth, where moths eat them and
rust destroys them, and where thieves break in and steal. Store
your treasures in heaven, where moths and rust cannot destroy,
and thieves do not break in and steal. Wherever your treasure is,
there the desires of your heart will also be.
—Matthew 6:19-21 (NLT)

*D*o you have a perpetual list of wants as I tend to have? I think about these things, hunt for them, and strategize to get them. Eventually I go in for the kill and purchase one of the items in question. It feels great! I'm excited . . . for a moment.

But with that want fulfilled, there is space in my life for the next want. And so, that wish list never really ends when I give it reign.

However, what I've come to learn is that all those "things" do not satisfy. Not at all. In fact, they lose their shine, go out of style, break, deteriorate, and are all too soon replaced by the next fad or newer technology.

Too many of us live our lives consumed by this unfulfilling cycle. We spend unfortunate amounts of time perusing thrift stores, fancy boutiques, garage sales, online shops, Etsy, or Facebook swap pages trying to get that next thing that will satisfy us and make us happy. That's not necessarily wrong to do, because we will naturally need to participate in commerce to provide for our families, but it can be quite shortsighted. It can certainly steal our contentment if we're not careful.

However, when we stretch ourselves to surrender what we want and exercise some difficult self-control, we simultaneously free up our finances to be more generous, to advance the kingdom of God in new ways, and to help those in need. With the same dollars we could use to spoil ourselves, we have the opportunity to make an investment that will endure.

I am not suggesting that it is evil to spend money on wants. I believe we have freedom to do that! Yet every time we consciously recognize the fleeting nature of the world, and sacrifice and leverage our finances for the people of God, we make a better choice. This is about more than saying no to a single want; rather, it's about breaking the power the wish-list cycle holds in our lives. It is about laying down our striving in favor of perspective and trust.

Embrace God's Word

For further insight, read Matthew 6:33; Philippians 4:11-13; and Mark 10:17-27.

Journal Your Thoughts

Is there something you want that God is calling you to let go of today?

What would it mean for you to take a break from your internal wish list?

The Idol of Happiness

Therefore, with minds that are alert and fully sober, set your hope
on the grace to be brought to you when Jesus Christ is revealed
at his coming. As obedient children, do not conform to the evil
desires you had when you lived in ignorance. But just as he who
called you is holy, so be holy in all you do.

—1 Peter 1:13-15

Reading fictional books and watching fictional movies tends to leave me with a niggling feeling of emptiness. While these portrayals are usually not very true to life, they do accurately represent some things. Movies reveal what we generally believe will make us okay, happy, and fulfilled as a culture. This includes things like being recognized, gaining wealth, having an adventure, falling in love, conquering an adversary, and achieving the big win. They are fun stories to follow along with, and they resonate with the human experience in many good ways.

However, too often, sin is justified to achieve "happiness." Revenge is taken. The disappointing husband is traded for Mr. Butterflies-in-Stomach. Personal glory is raked in by the handfuls. Characters pursue and achieve vain dreams. Certainly, there are movies that represent sacrificial love and uprightness, but the reason often hinges on the merits of the recipient or the power of humanity. These things do not ultimately hold water.

What comes after the picturesque wedding, the exciting escapade, or the epic sports victory? There is a reason why most stories end here. This is where the hard days of marriage, the consequences of sin, the disappointment of being forgotten, and the ache of eternity set in. The pursuit of our own happiness may be our "inalienable right" as humans, but it cannot satisfy that ache; it has no power to save us. At the end of the end, all our days spent running after happiness will vanish. Like the child who adamantly believes a diet of candy will make life good, so are we who pursue this mad goal. *To run after happiness is to chase the wind.* We think it will satisfy us, but it cannot.

The God who loves us unspeakably sees a much bigger picture. His chief goal is not that we be happy in this world. He has something far better in mind! That's why He commands us to *be holy as He is holy.* Real joy and lasting meaning flow from this holiness and obedience to God's calling.

If only we would trust that our Father sees things we do not, and just as a parent denies his child candy in favor of vegetables, grains, cheeses, and meat, so too God acts in love toward us when He calls us to deeper living. If only we would walk in obedience to the things He says and trust Him enough to make holiness our chief ambition and discover happiness as a sweet, sure, and complete by-product of that pursuit, we would discover something far better. May we lay our idea of "happiness" on His altar, and welcome confident hope that the reward for our faithfulness will be eternal, unimaginable joy.

Embrace God's Word

For further insight, read Ecclesiastes 2:1-11; 1 Peter 4:19; and Mark 10:29-30.

Journal Your Thoughts

How does your consumption of media shape your definition of happiness and success?

Is your own happiness king in your life, or do you trust God enough to make it seemingly secondary to living His way?

The Idol of Fairness

But if you suffer for doing good and you endure it, this is commendable before God. To this you were called, because Christ suffered for you, leaving you an example, that you should follow in his steps.

"He committed no sin,
and no deceit was found in his mouth."

—1 Peter 2:20b-22

*U*nfair treatment feels incredibly . . . unfair. When we perceive that our husband is not pulling his weight, when we do not get the nod we believe we deserve, when we notice that our life is more difficult than the life of our friend, or when we are excluded, it can be very upsetting. We want our interests in this world to be protected and honored, and we certainly do not believe we should receive this sort of repayment when we do good things for others!

However, all those feelings of frustration and entitlement do not take the eternal picture into account. They do not acknowledge and submit to what God has said: as Christians, we will suffer in this world, and it is to our credit if this suffering is a result of injustice (rather than wrongdoing). As we resolve to faithfully live in a manner pleasing to God, regardless of the outcome, we act as His children. *We follow the footsteps of Jesus, who*

> made himself nothing
> > by taking the very nature of a servant,
> ....

becoming obedient to death—
even death on a cross!

(Philippians 2:6-8)

Jesus did not demand His rights or pursue what was fair. Rather, He endured injustice from the very ones He had come to save, so He might obey the will of His Father. Through His humble submission, He brought redemption to the world. God was exalted all the more as a result of the injustice because it revealed His love in a way nothing else could.

Now, we have been commanded to follow in the footsteps of our Savior. This is the way of patient endurance and farsighted focus. When we feel unfairly treated, either by other people or by the life God has called us to live, we very well may be right. However, fairness is not the goal, and we must not be enamored with our own plight. We know that our lives will soon be over, and every opportunity we are given to exercise faithfulness and trust in this life will be to our credit in eternity. Even when circumstances don't feel fair, we still have the divine opportunity to walk in love. In this way, God is pleased with us.

Embrace God's Word

For further insight, read 1 Peter 3:14; Philippians 2:1-18; and 1 Peter 2:18-25.

Journal Your Thoughts

Do you feel unfairly treated in some way?

How can you exercise faithfulness and patient endurance in that situation?

The Idol of Loving the World

Do not love the world or anything in the world. If anyone loves the world, love for the Father is not in them. For everything in the world—the lust of the flesh, the lust of the eyes, and the pride of life—comes not from the Father but from the world. The world and its desires pass away, but whoever does the will of God lives forever.

—1 John 2:15-17

*A*s I pulled our mailbox open and caught sight of the bulging manila envelope, my heart lifted with excitement. It was my monthly Fair Trade Friday Club package. I held the other mail under my chin while my children jumped up and down eager to see what beautiful handmade items we would receive this month. And indeed, we were not disappointed when we pulled out a cheery, brightly colored bird mobile. As my kids held it up and admired it, I carefully inspected the printed tag tied on with a scrap of cloth. It told the story of the woman who had made it. Her name was Emily.

"Emily," the small piece of undyed cardstock explained, "is a self-taught artist and widow who lives in Nairobi, Kenya, in the slum of Kibera. She lives in a one-room house made of mud and sticks where she cares for thirteen children. Eight of them are her own, while the other five are her sister's kids. Her sister died of AIDS, and Emily and three of her children are HIV-positive." It went on to explain that, although aid programs provide her with free antiviral drugs to combat the illness, they leave her perpetually weak and tired. Even so, Emily leans on her faith in God for strength and does her best to provide for the children in her care through her artisan efforts.

That night as I lay in bed, I cast my eyes around my bedroom. I thought about how grateful Emily would be for just this one room—this one safe, dry, clean, quiet bedroom. Fourteen pallets would surely fit on this carpeted floor, not to mention the very comfortable king-sized bed and other furnishings. Suddenly, the whole rest of the house felt almost unbearably extravagant. And to think, I tend to want more.

Every day our western culture inundates us with the pull of the world. "Love me!" it entreats, demands, and finally, screeches. The status quo sets our expectations for our lives, and so we save up our money to have all the things we think we deserve with no thought to the implications of our stewardship.

But God is faithful, and He graciously reminds us of the apostle John's plea, "Do not love the world or anything in the world" (1 John 2:15). That is what Emily's story was for me. It was a reminder that there is something better than all my wants—something better than blind consumerism. It comes down to loving people with the dollars we spend and doing without so we can give more to those in need.

Here's the truth: "the world and its desires pass away, but whoever does the will of God lives forever" (v. 17). And so, we cut world-love out of hearts and thus free up our finances to love people instead. We advocate for organization like Fair Trade Friday and Grain of Rice Project, which redeem consumerism in powerful ways and connect the body of Christ internationally. And we reach out to meet needs with the extra God has provided for us, both locally and across the globe.

Embrace God's Word

For further insight, read Ecclesiastes 6:9 and 2 Corinthians 8:1-15.

Journal Your Thoughts

In what specific ways are you giving in to the lust of the flesh, the lust of the eyes, and the pride of life?

Is there an area God is calling you to exercise self-control by denying those desires in your life right now in order to better love others?

The Idol of Worldly Striving

"Everything is meaningless," says the Teacher, "completely meaningless!" What do people get for all their hard work under the sun? Generations come and generations go, but the earth never changes.

—Ecclesiastes 1:2-4 (NLT)

*B*ecause *life is as brief as an evening shadow,* all our worldly striving is meaningless. Our homes will be forgotten, our possessions will be wiped away, and our career accomplishments will cease to exist. Each of these treasures is nothing more than dust in light of eternity.

Think about the framework of the passage of time. We were once children. Now, almost as if in an instant, we find ourselves here. The past years have slipped through our grasp, and we are in the present moment. We once wondered what our future would hold, and now, here we are.

Perhaps we still wonder what life will be like in the future when our kids or grandkids are grown. In the same way, we will quickly see these outcomes behind us. Years come and go, and soon it will all be a distant memory.

Life is like a mist in the wind, yet too often we fail to recognize that we will all inevitably reach the end of our lives in a wingbeat of time. Before we know it, it will be over, and we will not have another opportunity to live a single moment. Because of this time paradigm, we might as well be there now, so quickly will it be upon us.

So, what do people get for all their striving under the sun? If this striving is devoted to status, money, comfort, and position, the answer is nothing. If their striving is defined by love for the Lord their God and neighbor, the answer is incomprehensible treasure.

The wise person considers these things and lives life with a clear mind, knowing and valuing the eternal over the glamor, glitz, and glory the world has to offer. The truth is there is more after this life than what we can see. *That's our hope*, and we must start living its truth now before it's too late!

Embrace God's Word

For further insight, read Psalm 102:11; Hebrews 6:16-20; and Matthew 6:19-21.

Journal Your Thoughts

What is one thing you tend to devote your life to that will not last?

What is one thing that will last?

The Idol of Nationalism

There is neither Jew nor Gentile, neither slave nor free, nor is there male and female, for you are all one in Christ Jesus.

—Galatians 3:28

$\mathcal{I}$t is easy to fixate on the pursuit of our own best interests as individuals and as a nation. We want peace and prosperity for ourselves, our neighbors, and our children. Those are good things, and it makes sense to desire and seek them.

However, as Christ followers, we must also remember that we are not better or more valuable because we are from a particular place. God loves and cares for the interests of all people, particularly those who love and follow Him. Eternity reminds us that the lives of our countrymen are not more valuable to God than the lives of others across the world. We recognize that, as John Piper put it, "we are more closely bound to those in Christ from other cultures than to our closest unbelieving compatriots."*

It is good to celebrate culture and heritage; these reflect the richness of God. It is good to respect those in authority; we are commanded to do this. It is good to work for safety and peace. And it is certainly good to be thankful for our nation and for the freedoms that we enjoy; each of these is a provision from our Heavenly Father.

However, at the end of time, we will be one with all other believers around the world. Geopolitical borders will cease to exist, or at least they will be quite different. Together, *people from every nation, tribe, people, and language will worship together before the throne of God.* This is God's ultimate

---

* John Piper, "Should Christians be Patriotic?" Desiring God, July 1, 2016, www.desiringgod.org/interviews/should-christians-be-patriotic.

goal, upon which we should set our hearts. It is the tangible picture of what we are working toward. When the divisions of the world begin to pull our hearts away, this image serves to realign us with God's vision.

Our physical country will not last forever. But we are part of a nation that will endure—"a chosen people, a royal priesthood, a holy nation" (1 Peter 2:9). *As believers, we are God's special possession, that we may declare the praises of Him who called us out of darkness and into wonderful light.* May we not make our nation an idol or hold onto it as a deficient substitute to the enduring hope we have been offered. May we instead serve Christ first and foremost and allow Him to guide our perspective.

Embrace God's Word

For further insight, read Revelation 7:9-10; 1 Peter 2:9-10; and Matthew 28:18-20.

Journal Your Thoughts

Examine your life: are you more committed to the well-being of the church worldwide or to the betterment of your political nation?

Why should the church be of greater concern?

The Wise Man Thinks About Death

A wise person thinks a lot about death,
while a fool thinks only about having a good time.
—Ecclesiastes 7:4 (NLT)

*I*f you knew you were going to die within a few months, would that change how you live now? For many people, it would. When we are forced to face our own mortality, our understanding of what is important shifts.

Different people have different reactions to this news. Some turn to pleasure. They strive to eat, see, do, and experience as much as they can before the flame of their life flickers out. They plan big trips and indulge themselves in many things, but none of it satisfies the ache of death. None of it could.

Others turn to relationships in their last days and surround themselves with loved ones, cherishing their moments together. These people treat family and friends with renewed kindness and appreciation. They attempt to soak in the very thing that is slipping through their fingers, but this is shrouded in grief for what will be lost. Legacy and the memories of others are their best hope of lasting meaning, but even this will soon be gone. This is the great tragedy of humanity under the sun.

However, in the face of death, there is a real hope available to those who would admit their need and reach out to God for salvation. Indeed, He is not far from any of us, and *He longs to draw us to Himself as a hen gathers her chicks under her wing, if only we be willing!*

As we allow the reality of death to take root in our hearts in the form of wisdom and unclouded perspective, our eyes will be opened to see the meaninglessness of the fleeting things we pursue. As a result, we will not hope in experiences or in relationships, although we will still seek to love and invest in those around us with our dying breaths. We will instead throw ourselves on the mercy of God and receive Jesus into the deepest parts of our hearts. We will live for Him from our very core, prostrating our lives at His altar and living in complete obedience to His Word. We will surrender ourselves to His will, and in this way, we will usher eternity into our lives.

In Christ, we are invited to press into our Heavenly Father and know true and lasting hope beyond this life. And that we must cling to!

The truth of the matter is this: whether or not we find ourselves young and in good health today or getting up in years and ill, our lives will end very soon in the scope of eternity. Everything I have described above is true right now.

Let's undistract ourselves from the endless pursuit of the world and take time to evaluate the brevity of life today, and thereby apprehend wisdom while there's still time.

Embrace God's Word

For further insight, read Matthew 23:37; 1 John 2:15-17; and Ecclesiastes 6:1-2.

Journal Your Thoughts

Do you live for this life, distracting yourself from the reality of death, or do you live with your heart set on heaven?

Why is it beneficial to consider death now? How does this process promote wisdom?

Section Two

Cultivating the Seeds of Eternity

A New Way of Seeing

Since, then, you have been raised with Christ, set your hearts on things above, where Christ is, seated at the right hand of God. Set your minds on things above, not on earthly things. For you died, and your life is now hidden with Christ in God. When Christ, who is your life, appears, then you also will appear with him in glory.

—Colossians 3:1-4

I Am the Lord's Servant

"I am the Lord's servant," Mary answered. "May your word to me be fulfilled." Then the angel left her.

—Luke 1:38

Mary, the mother of Jesus, was a normal teenage girl, but she was also special. We know that she was blessed among women and faithful to her calling, but what exactly did she do that was so noteworthy?

Well, as the story reads, she didn't *do* much of anything. Rather, she simply yielded herself to God's will. Things happened to her, but she mostly didn't do them. She didn't sign up to be the young, not-yet-wed mother of God's Son. What Mary did do was position her heart to believe God and trust His work in her. She accepted God's plan with a willing heart. Although she could not clearly see the bigger picture, she did not need to. She trusted God, knowing that He was worth any sacrifice.

We too must lay down our lives to receive God's will. Just as Mary did, we must acknowledge that we are His servants. Our lives are not our own, and when we hold our plans too tightly and seek to maintain stubborn control, we miss the point. We also miss the privilege of being part of something that truly matters.

When the angel of the Lord delivered the message of Christ's coming birth and her role as His mother, Mary had a profound response. She said, "I am the Lord's servant," and, "May your word to me be fulfilled" (Luke 1:38). God's plan for our lives is not likely to be easy or pain free, but it will be holy, glorious, and dripping with eternal purpose.

Take down the blinders of limited perspective today, and recognize that God's plan is much more wonderful than anything we could dream up. It spans across all of time and infinitely beyond. *God's thoughts are higher than our thoughts and His ways higher than our ways.* He is supreme over all creation, and *He will work everything together for the good of those who love Him.*

Let us release our stranglehold on life and open ourselves up to the will of God, whatever that may mean. There's no "doing" here, but instead there is surrender. There are open hands. Whether having more children, moving to Africa, or walking across the street to start a relationship with a neighbor, we are the Lord's servants; may it be to us as He wills.

Embrace God's Word

For further insight, read Isaiah 55:8-9; Romans 8:28; and Luke 1:26-38.

Journal Your Thoughts

How is God calling you to submission and trust?

Do you naturally envision yourself as God's servant? How does this posturing affect your outlook on life?

A Better Hope for Mothers

Therefore we do not lose heart. Though outwardly we are wasting
away, yet inwardly we are being renewed day by day. For our
light and momentary troubles are achieving for us an eternal
glory that far outweighs them all.

—2 Corinthians 4:16-17

Some seasons of mothering are harder than others. The sleep deprivation, the frustration, the realization of our own inadequacy, the crushing of our pride, the harder-than-we-wanted work, the many needs to be met, and the stretched-thinness of it all can cause our body and soul to react in ways we do not like and cannot control. We feel overwhelmingly exhausted, anxious, run-down, and emotional. We come to the end of ourselves, and we must cling to something.

All too often, in those difficult times, our best encouragement comes from the hope that "it will get better" or "this too shall pass." While I have clung to this type of hope many times, it has always felt shifty. This is an earthly type of hope—a statistical, optimistic wish. But in fact, we are not guaranteed that life will get better or easier. It may, or it may not. If that is the best hope we have, then our hope is not sound. This leads us to feel discontent and to wish our lives away, rather than embracing what God wants to do in and through us in hard moments.

However, gospel-hope offers something different entirely. Gospel-hope says that God is still good, even in the midst of our hardest hour. It says that God's grace is sufficient for us, right now. Gospel-hope says that these present sufferings will produce good fruit, fruit that cannot be borne in our lives otherwise. It says that we will be rewarded in eternity for our faithfulness in the troubles and that *these troubles themselves are producing* "an eternal glory that far outweighs them all" (2 Corinthians 4:17).

So let us lift our gaze from present hardships and cling to the hope that will not fail.

Embrace God's Word

For further insight, read Romans 5:3-5; James 1:2-4; and 2 Corinthians 12:1-10.

Journal Your Thoughts

Where do you most often find yourself seeking hope—in a better life or in heaven?

How does this gospel-hope impact your view of trails and hardships?

Not All Things Are Beneficial

"I have the right to do anything," you say—but not everything is beneficial. "I have the right to do anything"—but not everything is constructive.

—1 Corinthians 10:23

I am so grateful for the freedom we have in Christ! This freedom extends to anything that is not sin: eating good food, enjoying entertainment, buying nice things, reading a variety of books, and participating in all sorts of enriching, exciting, or fun activities whether or not they are temporary in nature. Our freedoms are truly glorious. We are not bound on these issues, and we should not let others bind us unduly. And yet, if we have doubts about anything, we must refrain completely, *for to violate our conscience is to sin.* And yet, if our action causes another to stumble in any way, we must not do it—so much greater is the eternal worth of a person's soul than our rights. Nonetheless, we can look around our world and see an abundance of good things that we can do as Christ followers.

As true as this is, Paul couldn't help but push the Corinthian church to think deeper. In spite of all our rights and freedoms to stretch our wings and experience this world as Christians, there is still yet a broader reality. *While everything is permissible, not everything is beneficial.* If we desire to add eternal significance to our days, we must pay attention to this dichotomy.

To choose the "just okay" stuff in place of the profitable is to make a trade-off, whether or not we mean to. This is not wrong, but neither is it best.

What then can our minds and hands find to do during our brief time on the earth that is beneficial? This means inviting God into our working and laughing and grieving. It means showing hospitality, encouraging others, and praying big prayers. It means working diligently within our homes, loving our husbands and children, and cultivating a state of awareness of God's presence in our lives. It means caring for those in need, sharing the hope of Jesus, and making real sacrifices to follow God. *It looks a lot like love.*

As we press into this God-life and learn to walk with Him throughout the moments of our day, we will naturally gravitate to beneficial things. And as we come to experience and realize the rich, abundant, and enduring depths God has made available to us in this life, we will gladly choose to invest our time in that which will endure.

Embrace God's Word

For further insight, read Romans 14:21-23; 1 Corinthians 10:31; and Galatians 5:13.

Journal Your Thoughts

Are you spending much of your life on something that falls into the "permissible but not beneficial" category? Write it here, and ask God to give you the long-sightedness and care to go deeper.

Complaining Put into Perspective

I consider that our present sufferings are not worth comparing
with the glory that will be revealed in us.

—Romans 8:18

Complaining has been a natural downfall for me throughout most of my life. I tend to take comfort in sharing my woes. Unfortunately, as I detail the difficulties of my life to whatever kind ear is available (difficulties such as the children who are pushing limits, the husband who works late, the fussy baby, the aches and discomforts of pregnancy, the ever-increasing grocery shopping bill, the endless household chores, and so on), not only do I fail to lift up the hearer but also I end up feeling sorrier for myself than ever! As I think about each aspect of my plight, I become increasingly enamored with my sufferings and less fixated on the sufficiency of Christ. I lose sight of the abundant life available to me in Him every day. Complaining does not serve me well.

I've come to see that complaining draws its very life from the root of wrong perspective. To think that life's small frustrations and disappointments are worth drawing undue attention is to believe that they are dominant over the blessings—both spiritual and physical—that God gives us each moment. This is not the case, and in fact, quite the opposite is true. *Christ came that we may have life, and have it to the full.* This was His expressed purpose, and He accomplished it. Now "our light and momentary troubles are achieving for us an eternal glory that far outweighs them all" (2 Corinthians 4:17)!

When our day does not go as we expected, we must remember, it went as God expected. Since we have abandoned our lives to Him so that we may find eternal life, why let these interruptions and difficulties perturb us?

Whether our day passes smoothly or progresses with difficulty should not be our chief concern. Our chief concern should be how God is at work in and through us and others in those moments.

As we learn to devalue our own plans, we will not feel so put out by life's difficulties. Instead, we will accept them willingly with open hands, eager to see what God will do in the midst of our struggle. We will find ourselves content simply to follow Him, taking one obedient step after another as He leads. Because we are functioning out of the well of His indwelling presence, we will not feel the need to grumble about inconveniences. Instead, we will share real struggles with friends with an undertone of gratitude, trust in God, and hope.

Let us nail our complaining ways to the cross, and instead meditate on and speak of His great grace, which is available and sufficient for all our trials and weaknesses. Let us use our small difficulties as an opportunity to boast in His goodness!

Embrace God's Word

For further insight, read John 10:10; Ephesians 4:29; and Philippians 2:14-16.

Journal Your Thoughts

Is there an area of your life where you tend to fall into complaining?

What specific changes can you make to avoid this?

Rise Up to Go Lower

My command is this: Love each other as I have loved you.
Greater love has no one than this: to lay down one's life for one's
friends.

—John 15:12-13

$\mathcal{E}$arly in my mothering journey, I was not prepared for the level of sacrifice that would be required of me. I enjoyed my new child immensely, but I also felt put out by the messes, limitations, and frustrations of caring for her. I still remember the night my husband dropped me off at home on his way to an evening work party. Our firstborn daughter was only three weeks old, and it was her bedtime. I was accustomed to being a part of these gatherings of colleagues and their spouses, and Mexican food sounded perfect. Yet, here I was, at home, nursing a tired infant by myself in a house that felt empty and lonely.

As she grew, new frustrations continued to surface. Meals went immediately into her hair and onto the floor, sleep was painfully interrupted far beyond my expectations, cleaning never ended, and tantrums felt like a morning-until-night occurrence. Each sacrifice that was required of me felt like a big deal. The truth was, I was not yet willing to fully embrace all that was required of me as a mother.

As one child became two, and two children became three, God slowly and graciously began the process of transforming my heart. As I read through the words of Jesus, I saw with new eyes His radical, countercultural message. Where the world would say, "Demand your rights," Jesus says, "Go lower." He didn't just teach this; He lived it! He lowered himself to identify with us, to serve us, to wash our feet, and to die for us. He loved us to the very end and beyond.

Now, He has commanded us to follow His example. When we lower ourselves to serve others, God's character is displayed in and through us. Likewise, when we immerse ourselves in God's love and learn to abide therein, we allow ourselves to be a conduit through which His love can freely flow. It is this divine love that will lead us into surrendered lives. *This is the very thing that proves we have passed from death into eternal life.* It is heavenly minded motherhood, just as God intended it.

In fact, this goes far beyond motherhood. When we follow Jesus, we learn what it means to lay down our lives in countless ways: for our neighbor, for our parents, for our friend.

Let us then fix our eyes on eternity and rise up to receive the ministry of our motherhood (and our living). May we know the joy of loving our families and all those around us as Christ first loved us.

Embrace God's Word

For further insight, read 1 John 3:16-20; Matthew 20:25-28; and John 13:1-17.

Journal Your Thoughts

How have you embraced motherhood to its fullest?

In what areas of your life have you held back and harbored resentment or self-pity in your serving? How can you let those things go?

Jesus Is Your Life

Jesus said to her, "I am the resurrection and the life. The one who
believes in me will live, even though they die."

—John 11:25

*I*t is natural to think about life in terms of priorities. As believers, we seek
to keep God first, of course, and then family, job, and other priorities follow
in line. We arrange our lives according to these priorities, assigning each
of them their share of time and energy. When we are on top of things, each
activity of our day fits into a neat compartment. While this can be a helpful
line of thinking when making decisions or establishing spiritual disciplines,
we must recognize that God is infinitely more than a line on our life's priority list.

In fact, God is our life itself! He is our source and our sustenance.
He infiltrates every moment we live through and every move we make. In
Christ, "all things were created: things in heaven and on earth, visible and
invisible, whether thrones or powers or rulers or authorities; all things have
been created through Him and for Him" (Colossians 1:16). He is the very
force holding each molecule in place. He is our bread of life. He is the reason
for our existence, and in Him each breath and passing moment finds its only
and total purpose. In Him is all truth. God is the crux of reality: "For He is
before all things, and in him all things hold together" (v. 17).

God is at work in every point of our day, and He invites us into con-
tinual, precious communion with Him. As we learn what it means to pray
continually and keep in step with the Spirit, and as we recognize our utter
dependence on God, He will expand our view of who He is. Suddenly our

God won't fit into a neat compartment in the big scheme of life; rather, we will recognize Him to be our life.

Let us not get so wound up in worldly perspective that we miss the truth of who we are and what our life is truly about. As followers of Christ, may we remember that *we died, and our life is now hidden with Christ in God. When Christ, who is our life, appears, then we also will appear with Him in glory.*

Embrace God's Word

For further insight, read Colossians 3:3-4; Galatians 2:20; and John 14:6.

Journal Your Thoughts

Is God merely a line on your priority list, or can you truly say that He *is* your life?

How does this (potentially) new mind-set change things for you?

The Good Things
God Wants for You

He who did not spare his own Son, but gave him up for us all—
how will he not also, along with him, graciously give us all things?
—Romans 8:32

*T*oday on the radio I heard a voice clip from a well-known Bible teacher. She said that God is good—He wants good things for His people—so we should believe that He will give us good things. The voice clip was just brief enough that I couldn't determine whether I agreed with her or not.

She certainly spoke truth. God is undeniably, exceedingly, and completely good. He does want good things for His people, and He gives us many good things. Yet perhaps sometimes our definition of *good* is something far less than what God has in mind. Perhaps our finite, limited view leads us to define *good things* in terms of health, popularity, and material abundance. And thus, we settle.

However, eternity begs a different perspective. Eternity dictates that all our wealth, health, ease, and worldly success are here today and gone tomorrow. And while these are good things in a temporary sense, they will not matter past the moment in which they are enjoyed. What's more, they do not bring about total dependence on God, and they do not drive us to throw aside everything to follow Jesus in complete surrender.

Could it be that there are better things in this life than the worldly blessings for which we busily pray and seek? Could it be that God is wiser, more loving, and more good than we know?

When we have the opportunity to be mistreated for the sake of the gospel, to faithfully persevere in trials, to return good for evil, and to radically and sacrificially give, we invest in eternity, glorify God, and store up treasures in heaven. All those days of comfort will hold no meaning.

So, *consider it pure joy when you face trials of many kinds because these trials lead us to higher places than we could have otherwise trodden.* Consider it pure joy when life is smooth, pleasant, and filled with the good things, recognizing that this too is a gift from God. Wisdom teaches us to "rejoice always, pray continually, give thanks in all circumstances" (1 Thessalonians 5:16-18), knowing that God is trustworthy and loving. He wants truly good things for the children He loves, including deep character, perfect dependence on Him, abiding joy not bound to circumstances, spiritual maturity, and rewards that will last forever.

Embrace God's Word

For further insight, read James 1:2-5; Romans 8:28-39; and 1 Peter 3:9-14.

Journal Your Thoughts

Before today, how would you have defined what it means to say God wants good things for me?

How does viewing life in the scope of eternity help you trust God in all things?

Significant Insignificance

"To whom will you compare me?
Or who is my equal?" says the Holy One.
Lift up your eyes and look to the heavens:
Who created all these?
He who brings out the starry host one by one
and calls forth each of them by name.
Because of his great power and mighty strength,
not one of them is missing.

—Isaiah 40:25-26

*T*his life is like a grain of sand on the beach. It is like a drop of water in the ocean. In fact, it is even less. It is infinitesimal in duration when compared to eternity, and therefore it is insignificant.

This earth, too, is incomprehensibly tiny against the backdrop of the universe. It is nothing but a speck within our massive galaxy, and our galaxy, too, is a speck within the vast breadth of space. It is one among an estimated 2 trillion other galaxies.* We are breathtakingly minuscule and inconsequential within our larger context.

And yet the God who created both time and space, the God who "stretches out the heavens like a canopy" and "brings out the starry hosts one by one, / and calls forth each of them by name," came to this earth (Isaiah 40:22, 26). He entered time. The infinite made himself finite. He became

---

* K. Hill, "Hubble Reveals Observable Universe Contains 10 Times More Galaxies Than Previously Thought," NASA, October 13, 2016, www.nasa.gov/feature /goddard/2016/hubble-reveals-observable-universe-contains-10-times-more -galaxies-than-previously-thought.

small, and then, He washed our feet. *Thus, He showed us the full extent of His love.* God breathed meaning into our lives on this earth. He bestowed significance to the insignificant.* Through His love, God made the flicker in time known as our existence actually matter.

Just as Christ died on this earth, and His death will ring out in heaven forever, so too will the choices we make during our time on this earth resonate. We have one chance to live our lives well, and we cannot begin to comprehend the lasting worth found in obeying God today. Nor can we comprehend the lasting grief found in following after our own sinful lust for the world. How foolish that we pridefully think we don't need God. May we have the eyes to see the truth of our need and the opportunity for significance God has placed before us!

Let us humble ourselves before our God and acknowledge that He is far bigger than we know, and let us thank Him for His love!

Embrace God's Word

For further insight, read John 13:1-17; Psalm 19:1-4; and Isaiah 40.

Journal Your Thoughts

How does the reality of your significant insignificance make you feel?

How does it change you?

---

* Louie Giglio, *Indescribable*, Passion Talk Series, directed by Six Step Records, 2012, DVD.

Rooted and Established in Love

*And I pray that you, being rooted and established in love, may
have power, together with all the Lord's holy people, to grasp how
wide and long and high and deep is the love of Christ, and to
know this love that surpasses knowledge—that you may be filled
to the measure of all the fullness of God.*

—Ephesians 3:17b-19

*T*o be filled to the measure of all the fullness of God takes one thing: being
rooted and established in His love.

It doesn't require a dream home. It doesn't require a loving husband,
nor a lucrative career, nor perfect children, nor any children. It does not
require a pain-free life, and it has nothing to do with us or *this decaying world
at all.* Rather, it has everything to do with Jesus and what He offers to us.

When we learn to believe, receive, and immerse ourselves deeply in the
love God has for us, only then *will we discover what it means to love Him in
return.* This divine love is constant through life and death, it spans heaven
and earth, and it persists both now and at the end of time. It is wider, deeper,
longer, higher, and more beautiful than we can fathom. It surpasses knowledge and *carries us out of fear.*

Instead of offering our hearts on the altars of this world (spouse, children, possessions, self), let us lose ourselves in a rich, consuming love relationship with God. As we do so, our lives will be permeated with that which
is wonderful beyond description: *the fullness of God.* This fullness is transcendent of all circumstances, space, and time. We simply cannot grasp the
power and significance of what has been made available to us. It is here now

for the taking, but we must lay aside our pride of sufficiency, insecurity, or unbelief to receive it.

Our family structure and possessions are temporary. In this world, they may be lost to us at any moment, and they certainly cannot save us. Therefore, let us learn what it means to cling to Jesus. May we be dependent on Him alone, and *may we be rooted and established in His love for us.*

Embrace God's Word

For further insight, read Romans 8:20-21 and 1 John 4:18-19.

Journal Your Thoughts

God loves you! Truly consider what that means. What does this simple but profound truth change in your heart?

How does the truth of God's love for you affect the way you approach your daily life? How about the way you view others?

Don't Forfeit Your Soul

What good is it for someone to gain the whole world, and yet lose
or forfeit their very self?

—Luke 9:25

*A*ccording to our fallen nature, we want to have our cake and eat it too. We want to retain our selfish ambitions, *and* we want God's guidance and presence in our lives. We want our image to remain intact, *and* we want Christ to acknowledge us before the Father. We want to maintain the controlling interest in our life now, *and* we want eternal life later.

But life with God doesn't work like that. In fact, *whoever wants to save their life will lose it, and whoever loses their life for Christ's sake will save it.* Jesus graciously spells this out for us in Luke 9, lest we deceive ourselves into thinking that ours is a genuine faith when indeed it is not. We must fear God, understanding that He is holy and not to be mocked. He does not owe us anything but has mercifully made a way for us to enter into new, eternal life with Him, washed white by His very blood. We should fall down in gratitude, giving our whole heart and life to Him with utter abandon!

Yet how often do we hold back? Even in the redeemed life, there is still a daily battle to be fought. This is why Christ exhorts us to *take up our cross daily and follow Him.* He knows we need to refocus every day. This race we're running is, after all, a marathon and not a sprint.

The world's offerings are deceptive and gross: fame, money, possessions, popularity, and self. Yet how easily these things wind their way around our human hearts. As we come to see life in light of eternity, we will more readily recognize how completely these pursuits miss the mark.

That's what faith does; it compels us to surrender everything so we might gain eternal life. As we believe and trust God's promises, we are overwhelmed with love and thankfulness. And thus, we stretch and grow and learn what it means to follow.

Embrace God's Word

For further insight, read Luke 9:23-26; Luke 14:25-35; and Matthew 10:28.

Journal Your Thoughts

Is there an area of your life you are withholding from God? Surrender it to Him!

What aspects of God's character empower you to surrender your life, even when it feels difficult?

Surrendering Possessions

The earth is the LORD's, and everything in it,
the world, and all who live in it.

—Psalm 24:1

One day, as Jesus was teaching, a young man approached Him. This man was eager to find eternal life. He had followed the Jewish law very closely, but he still lacked one thing. Because Jesus loved him, He told the man what he must do: "If you want to be perfect, go, sell your possessions and give to the poor, and you will have treasure in heaven. Then come, follow me" (Matthew 19:21). The heart-wrenching ending to this brief moment in time is that the young man *went away sad* because he was very wealthy. We don't know what he chose to do for sure, but it doesn't sound good for him.

When I read that account, something stirs in me. Our worldly possessions are insignificant, and if we have the opportunity to gain treasures in heaven by disposing of them, why wouldn't we? Many times, I've felt on the brink of coming to just such a conclusion. It would be so comforting to lay it down once and for all!

However, I have also seen what is perhaps an equally difficult calling in play. For some of us, selling all our stuff and giving the money away is exactly what God is stirring us to do. For others, He is calling us to retain our wealth with *the perfect perspective that it is God's and not ours*. There is something to be said for the daily discipline of presenting our possessions to God with open hands. This requires immense self-control, inner discipline, long-term effort, stewardship, and faithfulness, as opposed to a one-time, glorious act of obedience. In either way, we have the chance to make sacrifices for the kingdom of God.

Regardless, what earthly resources we have must be wholly committed to the Lord, ready to surrender at any moment as He directs.

Embrace God's Word

For further insight, read Matthew 19:16-30; Psalm 24:1; and Luke 12:33-34.

Journal Your Thoughts

What would it mean for *you* to completely surrender your possessions to Christ?

Is this easy for you, or difficult? Why?

Seeing Suffering in Light of Eternity

Very truly I tell you, you will weep and mourn while the world rejoices. You will grieve, but your grief will turn to joy. A woman giving birth to a child has pain because her time has come; but when her baby is born she forgets the anguish because of her joy that a child is born into the world. So with you: Now is your time of grief, but I will see you again and you will rejoice, and no one will take away your joy.

—John 16:20-22

*T*he reality of worldwide suffering (oppression, terrorism, abuse, illness, and poverty) grieves me deeply. I hear the stories. I see the news. I watch it unfold firsthand. In those moments, I ache for Jesus to return.

However, the good-news-truth is that all this suffering will one day be nothing more than a distant memory. Though the moments and days and years may seem unbearably long, they will very soon be eclipsed in the glorious presence of God as we, His followers, are swept up into eternity. As a mother knows, the pain of labor is forgotten almost as soon as the child is born and is replaced by new life, hope, triumph, joy, and an inexplicable chest-bursting love. In the same way, *the seemingly unbearable pain and sorrow of this world will give birth to irrevocable glory* as this present reality gives way to the full expression of God's glorious, eternal kingdom. This is our hope.

What's more, without suffering we get cozy with our life on earth. Without the harsh reminder suffering provides, we become content with our own sufficiency, status quo, and even sin. Suffering is the thing that turns us inside out before God, sets our gaze and hope on eternity, and teaches us to pray and long for a right-side-up reality. Suffering is the thing that undoes us in ways nothing else could. It's the thing that makes us *soft clay in the hands of the Master Potter,* and the thing that shows us our deep need for healing and redemption.

While we must feel the weight and pain of these realities for now as a result of sin, they will not have the last word. If we believe God for the unseen future we call eternity, *He promises that we will be renewed inwardly, day by day.* Hoping in heaven and putting feet to this promise is a glorious expression of confidence in what God has said to be true.

The reality of suffering presents an opportunity to exercise trust in God's eternal reality, unchanging promises, and absolute goodness. When we do not understand, and yet choose to trust, He is glorified in our lives!

Embrace God's Word

For further insight, read 2 Corinthians 4:16-18; Jeremiah 18:1-6; and Revelation 21:1-4.

Journal Your Thoughts

Do you tend to view suffering in this eternal light?

How does eternity breathe hope into suffering?

Offering Our Body "Image" as a Living Sacrifice

*Therefore, I urge you, brothers and sisters, in view of God's mercy,
to offer your bodies as a living sacrifice, holy and pleasing to
God—this is your true and proper worship. Do not conform to
the pattern of this world, but be transformed by the renewing of
your mind.*

—Romans 12:1-2a

*M*any women struggle with body image. I certainly have. The way we perceive our bodies and looks in these times of struggle is not favorable, and this negative perception leads us down many different, dark, and self-consumed roads. We may be insecure in our interactions with others and in our relationships. We may feel unlovable or self-conscious. We may spend hundreds of hours and dollars trying to overcome the way we look in order to diminish our feelings of anxiety and shame. We do not trust God's plan for how He made us to look.

However, as we elevate our perspective, one blessed by-product is a gradual release from inclinations toward this self-focused way of thinking. In light of eternity, we learn what it means to *present our bodies to God as a living sacrifice*. From there, we accept our situation (including looks) with trust, and allow God to live through us as He desires.

If the world does not perceive us as beautiful, we are in good company. *There was nothing desirable about Jesus's appearance*, and God's eternal purposes were fulfilled in Him to a degree beyond description. May we not be concerned with the finer points of our looks at all but instead believe that *what is mortal will be swallowed up in life!* We will indeed receive heavenly bodies.

In a parable, Jesus taught about a man who went on a journey. This man entrusted each of his servants with a sum of money and then left for a period of time. The faithful servants invested this money wisely and produced a return. The foolish servant buried it. In this parable, the master represents God, and we are His servants. Like those talents, God has entrusted us with a body, along with other types of resources. This body is *a tent* and a tool for multiplication within the kingdom of God. May we put it to good use, knowing that God has a plan for this exact face, body, and skill set for this time and place.

"We are God's handiwork, created in Christ Jesus," not to wow the world with how amazing *we* are, but "to do good works, which God prepared in advance for us to do" (Ephesians 2:10). We were created to deflect glory to our Lord. When we recognize that our bodies are temporary, we will learn to release them to God, embrace how He made us, receive joy, trust Him, and unabashedly use them as an instrument to accomplish His will.

Embrace God's Word

For further insight, read Isaiah 53:1-6; 2 Corinthians 5:1-10; and Matthew 25:14-30.

Journal Your Thoughts

Do you struggle with body image?

How would yielding your life and body to God completely affect your perception and treatment of your looks?

A Higher View

Set your minds on things above, not on earthly things. For you died, and your life is now hidden with Christ in God.

—Colossians 3:2-3

*O*ne day very soon, our possessions, successes, appearance, family unit, marriage, and everything we sought or worked for in this life will be gone like a wisp of smoke in the wind. Gone like the wildflowers. Gone.

This present reality is passing away.

So what value is there in striving for wealth or comfort? What real gain is there in vanity or selfishness or sin? There is none. Why then do we so fervently demand our rights and seek pleasure or happiness at the expense of godliness? Surely, these things are not the way of wisdom. Wisdom dictates that this life be lived with the next life in mind. For those who follow Jesus, there are things that do hold eternal value: loving others, obeying God, following His way of living, seeking Him, doing good, sacrificing for the sake of the gospel, privately praying, fasting, giving, loving our enemies, meeting the needs of others, withstanding trials and persecution, faithfully stewarding our resources, and laboring for God. These things are eternal, people's souls are eternal, and God's Word is eternal.

In light of these truths, parenting becomes less about giving our children every educational opportunity, advantage, and shiny thing and more about cultivating in them hearts that know and love God—*more about discipling them toward Christ.*

Our finances become less about gaining comfort and fun possessions and more about giving generously and demonstrating our faithfulness to

God's agenda for the world—*more about our allegiance to Him over material things.*

Our day-to-day living becomes less about having a good life and being happy and more about laying ourselves down on God's altar—*more about letting Christ live in and through us.*

Eternal perspective, by God's grace, raises our understanding of life *so that we may have spiritual minds to understand spiritual truths.* And yet living from a place of perspective takes daily discipline. So, when I feel myself starting to become entangled and distracted once again by the world right in front of my nose, I quietly remind myself, "It's all passing away," and my mind and heart shift back to spiritual truth. There is great solace and wisdom available in the light of eternity.

When we look through this lens, we will see trials differently. We will perceive hobbies, relationships, and money differently. And as we live eternal perspective day by day, we amass benefits that will span forever.

Embrace God's Word

For further insight, read Matthew 28:19-20; Matthew 6:24; Galatians 2:20; and 1 Corinthians 2:16.

Journal Your Thoughts

What stood out to you today?

How are you beginning to assimilate to a higher view of life as you journey through *Heavenly Minded Mom*?

Believing God

By faith we understand that the universe was formed at God's command, so that what is seen was not made out of what was visible.

—Hebrews 11:3

*A*ll of us have certain hopes for our lives. Perhaps we look forward to a good marriage, more children, health, dear friendships, a nice home, a relaxing retirement, or living to a ripe old age. Perhaps it is a certain level of comfort or family support that we expect. But what happens when one of those hopes is irreversibly crushed? What happens when we are abandoned by a spouse, unable to conceive, or diagnosed with a life-altering or terminal disease? What happens when the economy crumbles, a job is lost, or a loved one dies?

If our hope is anchored in this life, we will be overcome when these disasters befall us. However, we can know that this life and all it contains will not last. There are no guarantees here. This world is broken. Ultimately, it cannot deliver on its empty promises, and that's okay.

When we shift our gaze past the seen world and firmly place our longing in Christ, and when we allow this eternal *hope of heaven to anchor our souls,* everything changes. Now, we receive disappointments with steady confidence. We welcome God's promises from a distance, as Abraham did when he followed God's leading away from his homeland. Through this act of faith, God brought forth His salvation to the world, and yet *Abraham never received the fullness of that which had been promised to him before he died.* God's plan was far too great for this to materialize in just one lifetime: "Abraham believed God, and it was credited to him as righteousness" (Romans 4:3).

We trust that as we *endure the hardships of this life, God uses them to discipline and refine us* for His loving and good purposes. We believe Him for the things that we cannot see—the promises we have yet to receive. We trust that He will reward us as we earnestly seek Him, patiently endure, and simply obey His precepts and leading. We do not put our stock in this life, but rather we seek to surrender it to Him daily and in every regard. This is faith, and *it becomes the conduit through which God's saving grace my flow into our lives.*

Embrace God's Word

For further insight, read Hebrews 6:19-20; Hebrews 11:8-16; Hebrews 12:7; and Ephesians 2:8-9.

Journal Your Thoughts

Write a prayer asking God to help you firmly set your hope on heaven.

People in Light of Eternity

Then they will go away to eternal punishment, but the righteous to eternal life.

—Matthew 25:46

*A*s you go throughout your life, chances are you naturally cross paths with lots of people each day—fellow shoppers at the grocery store, pedestrians on the sidewalks, motorists driving in cars beside you, coworkers, waiters, bosses, children, and many more. In these exchanges, what do you see?

Do you look past them altogether, distracted by your errand? Do you see them as annoyances? Interesting stories? Resources or means to accomplish your goals?

There are four truths that I believe we should keep at the forefront of our minds when we are around other people: God made this person, this person bears His image, God loves this person, and this person will one day face judgment.

The world we know will very soon *be rolled up like a scroll*. In a span of time that is comparable to an instant, we will all find ourselves standing before our Creator. Every hidden thing will be made known, and *every knee will bow and tongue confess that Jesus Christ is Lord*. The sheep will be separated from the goats, and those who trusted in Christ will be whisked away and crowned with eternal life. Conversely, those who clung to sin or simply kept their lives for their own use and benefit on this earth (thus revealing they never truly trusted or knew Jesus for themselves), will be *banished into eternal punishment*.

This judgment is the imminent reality of each person. This should motivate us to be exceedingly patient with those around us, just as God is patient in His present provision of time, for He does not want "anyone to perish, but everyone to come to repentance" (2 Peter 3:9). It should motivate us to look on those who don't know Jesus with complete love and soul-wrenching compassion, being more concerned with their eternity than with our momentary interests, feelings, or convenience. Each individual we will ever encounter has a future past this world. He or she will spend eternity in God's presence or forever separated from Him.

People are precious to God. When He looks at them, He sees those He created in His very own image. He longs for each one to come to Him. We have the privilege of affecting the eternities of those around us simply by walking in obedience to God's calling. It is God's work, but He has chosen to use us as His instruments. We do this by exemplifying Christ in our lives, showing His love to those around us, and *always being ready to give an answer for the hope that we have.*

Embrace God's Word

For further insight, read Isaiah 34:4-6; Philippians 2:9-11; Matthew 25:31-46; and 1 Peter 3:15.

Journal Your Thoughts

Could your interactions with others use a dose of eternity? What specifically is God calling you to change about how you view them?

Did someone in your life impact your spiritual journey by showing this heaven-rooted love and grace to you?

Life Isn't the Ultimate Reality

For now we see only a reflection as in a mirror; then we shall see face to face. Now I know in part; then I shall know fully, even as I am fully known.

—1 Corinthians 13:12

*I*n my deepest meditations about reality, eternity, and the kingdom of God, I began to perceive life almost as if it were a dream. I recognized that the world I saw was not the ultimate reality. These finite things would soon be gone and little remembered. I saw that in a breath of time, everything seen would pass away, and we would wake up in eternity.

Of course, this physical life is very real, and in fact, *we will be held accountable for every empty word we have spoken.* What's more, the spiritual implications of Christ's sacrifice and the redeeming, epic work of God in this world will be held up in honor forever. *Even the angels long to look into these things,* so gut-wrenchingly wonderful is the enduring love of God as displayed in this world through the gospel!

Our lives will bear eternal consequences, which hinge on our faith in Christ during our brief lives on this earth. Yes, this life matters greatly—not for the new outfit we splurged on, and not for the promotion our husband got at work but for the way we posture our lives, with our face to the ground and our arms outstretched at the foot of the cross. There is a more vibrant and enduring reality at hand. It is right here, today, and it will be our reality forever. *This reality has been set in our hearts,* and its truth must permanently and completely affect everything we do and see on this earth lest we waste our lives.

This way of perceiving life, almost as if it were a dream or, in the words of Paul, *as if gazing through from the other side of a mirror,* changes things. A healthy measure of detachment from the world frees us from subservience to our circumstances and emotions. By seeing this world as a subreality to the eternal, we won't be able to help but to take things less personally and more as Christ would. When we remove ourselves from hard and good things, we will take on God's perspective and minister out of His grace according to His will, disregarding our own will as foolish. In this way, idols will fall to the ground, and we will learn what it means to live in faith.

This is how we live a life that matters.

Embrace God's Word

For further insight, read Matthew 12:36; 1 Peter 1:10-12; Ecclesiastes 3:11; and 1 Corinthians 13:9-13.

Journal Your Thoughts

Take some time to pray and reflect. As you journal, ask God to open your eyes to His ultimate reality.

The Power of Faithful Stewardship

And I will do whatever you ask in my name, so that the Father may be glorified in the Son.

—John 14:13

George Müller was a minister in nineteenth-century England. He noticed the people who surrounded him did not expect God to answer their prayers or do anything unusual in their midst. Müller yearned to teach them about God's faithfulness and power, so he came to an amazing decision. Rather than make his needs known when he felt God leading him into a particular ministry, he simply prayed in secret, telling God the needs, and watched to see what God would do. Over and over again, miraculously, God met each of them!

By the end of his life, Müller had distributed more than $8 million, much of which was given to him in answer to prayer. He started the Scriptural Knowledge Institute and built four orphanages, which had served and housed a total of ten thousand children by the end of his life. He devoted himself to the things God called him to do, yet his personal possessions were valued at only $800 at the time of his death.*

I think it's safe to say that George Müller did not set his sights on this world. Because he saw the bigger picture, he was able to sacrifice and steward money and resources for the sake of the kingdom without becoming greedy

---

* H. T. Blackaby, *Experiencing God: How to Live the Full Adventure of Knowing and Doing the Will of God* (Nashville: Broadman & Holman, 2008).

or self-interested. God accomplished great things through him as a result. The more I learn about Müller's life, the more I want to be like him.

It is all too easy to fall into the wealth-accumulation, earth-focused mind-set. This is where many people live with little clue that there is far more to the equation. To live a life of eternal significance is to forge a new way, and to make choices that have nothing to do with our gain and everything to do with God's promises and call. As we press into eternity, may God open our eyes to clearly see what it means to lay down our comfort, our lust for things, and our cushy retirement goals.

May we ask God with boldness to make us a faithful funnel for resources, not with sticky fingers, but with complete trust and obedience. Let us learn what it means to pray big prayers in faith and to live our lives at full tilt for the kingdom to our dying breath.

Embrace God's Word

For further insight, read Matthew 6:19-21; 1 Timothy 6:17-19; and Matthew 6:31-33.

Journal Your Thoughts

What holds you back from fully committing your life and financial resources to God?

How do examples like that of George Müller challenge and inspire you?

Two Secrets to a Satisfied Life

I am not saying this because I am in need, for I have learned to be content whatever the circumstances. I know what it is to be in need, and I know what it is to have plenty. I have learned the secret of being content in any and every situation, whether well fed or hungry, whether living in plenty or in want. I can do all this through him who gives me strength.

—Philippians 4:11-13

Striving for success, recognition, wealth, a better this-or-that, and more, more, more is an empty use of a precious life. These things are alluring, yet they cannot satisfy us.

This week I saw a motivational sign in a store that read, "Life is short, so hurry up." It saddened me to think of all the lives that are spent hustling for things that will not last.

Solomon sums it up so well:

This too is a grievous evil:

As everyone comes, so they depart,
    and what do they gain,
        since they toil for the wind?
All their days they eat in darkness,
    with great frustration, affliction and anger.

(Ecclesiastes 5:16-17)

Take a moment to examine your own life. Is your focus solely on improving your circumstances, having more, or imagining the next thing you'll accomplish or acquire? Do you experience *the frustration, affliction, and anger* that Solomon identified when you come up short? Or do you have the wisdom to seek contentment right where you are? Are you willing to simply be where God has you, in sweet fellowship with Him? It is the latter that brings freedom and happiness. Contentment is the first secret to a satisfied life.

But even if we discover contentment, our life could still be pretty meaningless. We will eventually die, and all the happiness and earthly fulfillment we found through contentment will be nothing but a wisp of smoke in the wind, although our faithful trust in God will remain.

Yet there is another thing—this other component of living a satisfied life—that brings eternity even more fully to our days. At the very end of the Book of Ecclesiastes, Solomon sums up his teachings and wisdom with these sentences:

> Now all has been heard;
>> here is the conclusion of the matter:
> Fear God and keep his commandments,
>> for this is the duty of all mankind.
>> (Ecclesiastes 12:13)

Of all the glorious things you may want to do for God, what He actually wants is your reverent obedience. Obedience is the second secret to a fulfilled life—obedience, that is, to living God's way and following His lead throughout your life. If we seek contentment and walk in obedience to God, we will discover what it means to live a truly satisfied life, both today and eternally.

Embrace God's Word

For further insight, read 1 Timothy 6:6-7; John 8:51; and James 1:22-25.

Journal Your Thoughts

What do you need to let go of today in order to pursue contentment?

How can you take a next step of obedience in your life right now?

The Lost Art of Fearing God

The fear of the LORD is a fountain of life,
turning a person from the snares of death.
—Proverbs 14:27

Our generation is losing the art of fearing God. It is out of fashion. The idea of fearing God does not have that feel-good draw. And since it is hard to understand, we choose to put it out of our minds, and thus, we miss eternal truths. We idolize ourselves and grow fat on a skewed perception of grace. The effects of this shift are wriggling their way into the cracks of our society, and we are seeing the crumble all around us.

I wonder, have we given up on reading the whole Bible—on reading it honestly? The truth is, God's love and grace must be understood in the context of His holiness and justice. One gives the other its power and meaning, and both aspects of God are equally true and important.

God is not our grandpa in whose eyes we can do no wrong. He's not a teddy bear. He is love, but we must remember that this love is a fiery, fierce, and jealous love. He is holy, and far more so than we could possibly acknowledge. A lack of understanding of His character will lead us to live mushy, ineffective, wasted lives, yet "fear of the LORD is the beginning of wisdom, / and knowledge of the Holy One is understanding" (Proverbs 9:10). Through learning to properly know and fear God, we will have the understanding and wisdom we need to live a rightly divided and discerning life: "The LORD confides in those who fear Him" (Psalm 25:14). Then will we know the truth.

As I have grown in my understanding of God and His word, I better process my sin in light of His holiness. This leads me to take it seriously! I repent those sins to Him, and when I realize that He is not to be trifled with, I'm far more able to stay the course marked out for me. My clear-eyed view of my own wretched state leads me to see the gravity of what He has done for me on the cross. This humbles me. It makes me exceedingly grateful. A growing and reverent understanding and fear of God is an important safeguard to help us keep from sinning, as is a growing and reverent understanding of His love and mercy.

God's grace will mean more to us when we feel the weight of our sin. When we fail to fear God, we inadvertently minimize both our sin and His holiness.

Today, let's seek to know God wholeheartedly—diving into the Bible to know Him completely.

Embrace God's Word

For further insight, read Job 28:28; Philippians 2:12-13; and Matthew 10:28.

Journal Your Thoughts

Do you fear God? If not, how would implementing this act of reverence change your everyday actions?

Spend time worshiping God by proclaiming His holiness back to Him in a written prayer.

The Blessedness of Less

Two things I ask of you, LORD;
do not refuse me before I die:
Keep falsehood and lies far from me;
give me neither poverty nor riches,
but give me only my daily bread.
Otherwise, I may have too much and disown you
and say, "Who is the LORD?"
Or I may become poor and steal,
and so dishonor the name of my God.

—Proverbs 30:7-9

*I*t is not godlier to have less, neither is it godlier to have more. Our spiritual life is not a matter of our possessions. Sometimes the workings of God are mysterious and wonderful, and He can use a situation of less to bless us just as He can use a situation of more. The things of God are exceedingly deeper than face value.

Too often we mistakenly think this life is what matters—our daily comfort, our temporary happiness, our worldly appetites. We look around at our material possessions, and, instead of gratitude, we feel discontentment and dissatisfaction. We think we need more. Suddenly a closet full of clothes isn't enough. A warm place to call home isn't enough. That car, those shoes, these furnishings—insert anything—are not enough.

It is not wrong to have or buy things. Rather, it is the state of our hearts that matters. Sometimes that ability to buy, buy, buy is a great enemy of contentment. Sometimes God protects us from ourselves, knowing that "having it all" will lead our hearts away from Him by distracting us or, worse, weaseling in even deeper and becoming an idol. This is when God lovingly sets a boundary.

Other times God withholds the good stuff to give us the best stuff. Through seasons of less, He develops depths of trust, faith, patience, and contentment that we could not know otherwise. This is the true treasure. This is where the deep blessing lies. These are the things that hold true value.

There is a blessedness in having the things of the world. It is God who faithfully meets our needs and gives us good gifts. But there is also a blessedness in not having it all. Contentment is worth far more than wealth. *We must not love money, for Christ has said He will never leave us,* and He is exceedingly sufficient! "We brought nothing into the world, and we can take nothing out of it" (1 Timothy 6:7), so let us instead pursue godliness with contentment. Let us trust God and value spiritual blessing over the stuff of the world. *In this, there is much gain!*

Embrace God's Word

For further insight, read Hebrews 13:5; Philippians 4:11-13; and 1 Timothy 6:6-11.

Journal Your Thoughts

Whether you feel you "have it all" today or not, choose gratitude and recognize God's goodness. Trust His wisdom. Write a note of thanks for giving you exactly what you need.

Obedience Is Costly

For whoever wants to save their life will lose it, but whoever loses their life for me will find it.

—Matthew 16:25

When we position our lives to follow Jesus in all things, it will cost us everything: our sin, our plans, our will, our ambitions, our comfort, our prejudices, our money . . . everything. This is the simple formula for discipleship: *we must lose our life to find it.* Convenient faith is empty and will not save us. We cannot have both the world and Christ, though many have convinced themselves otherwise. *Just as the builder counts the cost before starting a project, so must we count the cost of following Jesus,* and it is very costly indeed.

But what about when our obedience is costly not just to us but to those around us? Is this cause for alarm? Should this curb our willingness to follow Jesus wherever He leads?

I recently heard the story of a couple who moved to Asia to do mission work. During that time, their six-year-old daughter was bitten by a mosquito, which resulted in an incurable, life-altering disease.

My heart aches for this family. Obedience was costly to the parents. They chose to leave the many comforts of home, halted their lives, took huge risks, and endured many hardships for the sake of the kingdom of God. But it was also costly to their children, who experienced sacrifice because of their parents' obedience.

What do we do with stories like this? Do we balk at following God? No, we must not. Although it is our holy task to care for our children well, we must always be ready to entrust them to God. When difficult things happen, we cling to His promise: *that after we have persevered under trial and stood the test, we* "will receive the crown of life that the Lord has promised to those who love Him" (James 1:12). And His other promise: "in all things God works for the good of those who love him, who have been called according to his purpose" (Romans 8:28). God is sovereign, and we can trust His plan even when we do not understand it.

Embrace God's Word

For further insight, read Luke 14:25-33 and Revelation 2:10.

Journal Your Thoughts

Are you willing to obey Jesus regardless of the cost? Take time right now to work through this with Him, journaling your thoughts below.

Longing for Redemption

For God is not a God of disorder but of peace—as in all the congregations of the Lord's people.

—1 Corinthians 14:33

*I*t is summertime here, the season of yard work and heat, of blue skies and sunshine. There is a house I drive by often. It is charming with an always-neat lawn and beautiful, well-watered landscaping. I look over to appreciate and enjoy the sight of it every time I pass by. It soothes me—something beautiful and immaculate in the midst of a sun-scorched, overgrown, and chaotic-feeling world.

Why are these glimpses of near-perfection so compelling? I believe it is because deep in our hearts, *this* is what we were made for. Rightness, order, and untainted beauty proclaim God's original design for creation, which was good. *In fact, it was very good.*

As we know all too well, the story took a hard-right turn when sin entered the picture. Through *the ensuing curse of death*, things quickly began to unravel. Now we live under the affliction of frustration, pain, toil, and disappointment. But yet it is these very realities that drive our souls to long for the redemption of the world. Creation's subjection to futility is not futile. By God's grace, this was done so that creation itself might "be liberated from its bondage to decay and brought into the freedom and glory of the children of God" (Romans 8:21). And indeed, *Jesus is making all things new.* The story of creation, rebellion, and redemption is the unfolding of the ultimate epic poem, infinite in symbolism, and boundless in depth and joy.

And so, the work of making something neat and right in this world, when done unto the Lord, can be worshipful and holy. These things touch our souls and cry out for the perfection that was lost and the redemption that is yet to come. Now, when I neaten my home or weed my flower beds, I do it in an attitude of worship. This changes the paradigm completely in those moments. Simple tasks transition from mundane and menial to sacred offerings to the Lord.

We are physical beings, and God is compelling us to experience who He is and what He is doing in our world in tangible ways. Let's join Him there.

Embrace God's Word

For further insight, read Genesis 1:31; Genesis 3:16-19; Romans 8:18-25; and Revelation 21:1-5.

Journal Your Thoughts

How do you experience God through the hard work of making things orderly and beautiful?

How can you make these actions more intentionally worshipful?

Grace and Peace in Frustrations

You will keep in perfect peace
those whose minds are steadfast,
because they trust in you.

—Isaiah 26:3

*U*nfortunately, stressed-out is my go-to posture when dealing with life's little frustrations. From my two-year-old daughter's frequent spills and accidents, to the massive couch cushion fort my older children love to create at the most inopportune moments, to my looming writing deadlines, to the unending work of running a home and caring for little children, I have no shortage of things to keep me frazzled. In many different ways, I add drama to my frustrations to justify self-pity.

This is not the life God is calling any of us to live; His way is quite the opposite. In the midst of life's frustrations, we have the choice to indulge ourselves in tension and stress or to trust God and enjoy His presence and sufficiency each moment and rely on His leading and wisdom. When we see eternally, we will realize that God is sovereign and big, *these troubles are light and momentary*, and all our agitation amounts to very little.

Rather than get bent out of shape by the daily grievances inherent in this broken world, all we need do is to trust God and obey what He is calling us to do moment by moment. So, when our favorite piece of furniture is marred or broken by a rambunctious child, we take steps to discipline and remedy, not because the furniture is important (it's not) but because the child is important. We've been entrusted with the job of training him so that he may know God and make Him known eternally. And when our day feels like a complete disaster as one child dumps over a box of uncooked spaghetti while another emerges covered in diaper rash cream as we are trying desperately to get out the door on time, we keep perspective that schedules can be changed. When we discover that our little one has managed to experimentally flush our phone down a toilet, which is now clogged—even yet, we retain within ourselves a measure of grace. In each of these instances, we can find peace knowing that God allowed or even orchestrated all these things for His glory. We trust that He is up to something, that He will provide, and that the best is yet to come.

When we learn to *fix our eyes not on what is seen but on what is unseen*, we will apprehend God's *perfect peace*. When we discover what it means to function from a place of heavenly mindedness, allowing the *God of peace to equip us* for our daily work, our joy will be unquenchable: "And the God of all grace, who called you to his eternal glory in Christ, after you have suffered a little while, will himself restore you and make you strong, firm and steadfast" (1 Peter 5:10-11). Let us fix our eyes on God's goodness and the redemption that is to come.

Embrace God's Word

For further insight, read 2 Corinthians 4:16-18 and Hebrews 13:20-21.

Journal Your Thoughts

Do you tend to dramatize life's frustrations or take them in stride?

What is one small frustration in your daily life that could benefit from the practice of the disciplines of grace, perspective, and peace?

Blessed Surrender

The steadfast love of the LORD never ceases;
his mercies never come to an end;
they are new every morning;
great is your faithfulness.
"The LORD is my portion," says my soul,
"therefore I will hope in him."

—Lamentations 3:22-24 (ESV)

*W*e got the news on a bright, beautiful winter morning: a family we knew had been in a car crash. A tractor-trailer had lost control on icy roads, crossed the median, and hit them not once but twice. We prayed fervently, yet several hours later, their thirteen-year-old daughter died from her injuries. It started out as just a normal day, yet somehow this firstborn little girl was gone.

What do we do with the reality of suffering and loss in our world—with the reality that it may come to our doorstep at any moment? What do we do with the fact that *we are destined to die,* along with each of our loved ones, lest Jesus come back first? What do we do when it actually happens to us or someone around us?

When we look at life in view of eternity, we have hope—such wonderful hope! We understand that thirteen years pass in the blink of an eye, as do one hundred years. *Our time here is but a shadow,* no matter how many or few our years may be. Of course, we will still experience heaviness and pain, but in the midst of even the darkest moment, there is great hope.

When our hope is anchored in heaven, we have the ability to surrender our children, our loved ones, and our own lives into God's hands. We cannot control suffering and death, but we can know that God is good, sovereign, wise, merciful, and loving. We can trust Him to be the gatekeeper of all our circumstances, knowing that His grace will be sufficient for it all. He holds the whole scope of our eternal existence in His loving hands.

While these parents will grieve for the rest of their days on this earth, those too will soon be over. Glory and redemption will eclipse this sorrow, just as the most brilliant sunrise eclipses the dark of night. Our hope in Christ is profound and complete. It spans the grave and is not dependent on this shifty and uncertain world. May the name of the Lord be praised!

Embrace God's Word

For further insight, read Hebrews 9:27; Job 8:9; Philippians 3:10-14; and Revelation 21:4.

Journal Your Thoughts

Where is God calling you to let go of trepidation and anxiety over potential future suffering or loss?

Where have you already experienced suffering in your life? How can you allow God to breathe hope into your pain?

Most to Be Pitied

*For if the dead are not raised, then Christ has not been raised
either. And if Christ has not been raised, your faith is futile; you
are still in your sins. Then those also who have fallen asleep in
Christ are lost. If only for this life we have hope in Christ, we are
of all people most to be pitied.*
                                                        —1 Corinthians 15:16-19

*D*o you live in such a way that you would be the most pitied of all people
if your hope of eternal life were not true? According to Paul, this should be
the mark of a believer. We lay down our lives and take up our cross to follow
Christ. We fix our eyes on the things above, and, just like Moses, we *choose
to be mistreated and endure disgrace for the sake of Christ, rather than enjoy the
fleeting pleasures of sin, because we are looking ahead to our reward.* We put all
our chips in the basket of eternity—so much so that our lives would be futile
and tragic apart from this faith of ours proving true.

Wonderfully, the validity of this hope is not in doubt. God has con-
firmed it by marking us "with a seal, the promised Holy Spirit, who is a
deposit guaranteeing our inheritance until the redemption of those who are
God's possession" (Ephesians 1:13-14). Because we know that Christ was
raised from death and that we too will be raised, we have the power to surrender our lives to Him completely.

Sadly, however, some believe we can have everything the world has to
offer and eternal life later. We live a great life by the world's standards that
requires no sacrifice, indulging ourselves as we will. We do not fear God,
and we assume that He will accept us on our terms. May we not be so callous
and prideful!

Let us instead stand in awe of our holy God, recognizing that *He is a consuming fire and a jealous God.* May we so confidently believe in our eternal life that we put this belief into action—that's genuine faith! May we give our lives over to our Heavenly Father to the final drop and allow Him to accomplish His will through us. Let us stake all we have and all we are on the truth of the Resurrection.

Embrace God's Word

For further insight, read 1 Corinthians 15:12-19; Hebrews 11:24-26; and Deuteronomy 4:24.

Journal Your Thoughts

By examining your life, how do you live in such a way (completely and sacrificially devoted to Christ) that you would be most pitied of all people if this hope of eternal life were not true?

Where do you fall short of this standard?

In Christ Alone

All streams flow into the sea,
yet the sea is never full.
To the place the streams come from,
there they return again.
All things are wearisome,
more than one can say.
The eye never has enough of seeing,
nor the ear its fill of hearing.

—Ecclesiastes 1:7-8

*N*othing in this world can fill the emptiness and satisfy the deep long-ings in our restless hearts. The more we try to usher fulfillment into our lives by nonspiritual means, the more disillusioned and empty we will be. We are thirsty, parched, and dying for real meaning, and in place of life-giving water, we too often consume the goods of the world, which offer a momen-tary high but ultimately let us down lower than ever. They accomplish less than nothing to meet and fulfill the longings of our hearts.

Yet God, by His grace, *has* "set eternity in the human heart" (Ecclesiastes 3:11). He desires for us to turn toward Him and find Him. He graciously beckons us into eternal life, and this eternal life gives avenue to *an eternal way of seeing life.*

As we set our sights on heaven and intentionally cultivate this perspec-tive in our lives, we naturally *lay our bodies, actions, and livelihoods down as a sweet sacrifice on God's altar.* When we purpose to follow Him at any cost, *knowing we will receive an inheritance that will not perish, spoil, or fade as our reward,* He moves into our lives in power. Because He made us, He is the

One who is able to bring us into eternal life. He is also able to help us recognize our potential as the women, neighbors, servants, wives, leaders, and mothers He created us to be. There can be nothing more fulfilling to our hearts than to open up our lives to obediently seek and follow God's perfect will. Through this surrender we will know what it means to be completely right. May we not allow our lives to pass by never knowing this rich blessing.

When we die to ourselves in order to follow Christ, we gain immeasurable treasure both for now and for eternity. This death happens when we receive Him, but it must also happen daily as we follow after Him.

Embrace God's Word

For further insight, read Colossians 3:1-3; Romans 12:1; and 1 Peter 1:3-9.

Journal Your Thoughts

Write a prayer asking God to open your eyes and show you if there is an area in your life where you are wrongfully seeking fulfillment in that which will not truly satisfy.

Love Never Fails

For Christ's love compels us, because we are convinced that one
died for all, and therefore all died. And he died for all, that those
who live should no longer live for themselves but for him who
died for them and was raised again. So from now on we regard
no one from a worldly point of view.
                                                    —2 Corinthians 5:14-16

*W*e are made in the image of God. Because of who He is, all humans have a certain capacity to love. However, because of our fallen nature, this love is imperfect and easily tainted.

Why else do so many starry-eyed newlyweds find themselves in a world of disillusionment, heartache, or divorce? Why else do we lose our temper and patience with our children? We say we love our families unconditionally, but we are fickle and weak in our own power. How much of our love is rooted in the self-focused desire to receive their love in return? How much of our love is rooted in a desire for the approval of the world? We want others to see us as a loving wife and mom, so we do the loving wife and mom things.

If you peel back the layers, our human love is often more about us and more conditional than we realize. We fall in love with our husbands because they give us attention and make us feel valued and loved. We love our children because we get to be important and needed, and we receive love, companionship, and acceptance in return. While that is part of God's design, pure love flows directly from the endless reservoir of our Heavenly Father. We desperately need His help to love even our husbands and children, let alone that hard-to-love in-law or coworker. This must start with the gospel, with the regeneration of our hearts, and with the acceptance of God's love for us. It is only in Him and through Him and by His power that we dip our ladle into the life-giving, holy, and eternal waters of love. This is a fruit borne by His Holy Spirit in us!

How do we know if we are loving those around us, be it our own family or the stranger we pass by on the sidewalk? This is the test: "Love is patient, love is kind. It does not envy, it does not boast, it is not proud. It does not dishonor others, it is not self-seeking, it is not easily angered, it keeps no record of wrongs. Love does not delight in evil but rejoices with the truth. It always protects, always trusts, always hopes, always perseveres. Love never fails" (1 Corinthians 13:4-8).

Embrace God's Word

For further insight, read 1 John 4:16-21 and 2 Corinthians 5:14-21.

Journal Your Thoughts

How can you grow in truly loving your husband today? Your children? Your coworkers or neighbors?

How are you exercising genuine love toward others?

The Faith to Forgive

Forgive, and you will be forgiven. Give, and it will be given to you.
A good measure, pressed down, shaken together and running
over, will be poured into your lap. For with the measure you use, it
will be measured to you.

—Luke 6:37b-38

*F*orgiveness is perhaps one of the most beautiful, difficult, and holy things we have the privilege and responsibility to do on this earth. It is both a reflection and an affirmation of what Christ has done for us. Our debt of sin and rebellion against God is unfathomably great, and yet He offers us pure and complete forgiveness by His grace through faith in Jesus.

Forgiveness has nothing to do with the merits of the recipient and everything to do with love. It is an opportunity for us to put our stake of trust in the ground. As we follow God in this cosmic act of faith and obedience, we give up our rights just as Christ did, testify to what He has done, and acknowledge our own sinfulness before God.

Whether or not to forgive those who have wronged us is not a choice with which Jesus left us. Over and over again He taught us, *forgive and you will be forgiven.* We must fear God and take Him at His word!

In our limited view, the offenses committed against us and our loved ones may seem to be of insurmountable proportions. But if we could only zoom out, we would soon realize that the worst harm or wrong done against us in this life is nothing in comparison with our own offense against God, because of His absolute holiness! Yet *He is kind to the unthankful and to those who are wicked*, and we must be like Him.

Forgiveness flows from faith in the God who commanded us to give it. As we give, so shall we receive, *and the measure we use will be measured to us.*

Embrace God's Word

For further insight, read Matthew 6:14-15; Matthew 18:21-35; and Luke 6:27-38.

Journal Your Thoughts

Do you believe God enough to forgive freely as you have been forgiven? If you need to forgive someone in your life, don't delay! Start by writing his or her name along with a prayer asking God to help you do just that.

Releasing the Past

But one thing I do: Forgetting what is behind and straining
toward what is ahead, I press on toward the goal to win the prize
for which God has called me heavenward in Christ Jesus.
—Philippians 3:13b-14

*H*ave you ever said or done something that was hurtful to someone else, whether intentionally or not? When we are confronted with the hurt we've caused, we might feel defensive. Or, if we truly love this person, and if he or she is sincere and humble in approach, what we probably feel most is instant and deep regret and sadness. Unfortunately, in those moments, we cannot unsay the thing we've said or undo the hurt we've caused. All we *can* do is to ask for forgiveness and resolve within ourselves to do better next time. The other, in turn, must do the forgiving.

I've experienced many such exchanges within my marriage. This relationship, more than any other, has exposed my selfishness and callousness. When my husband gently confronts me, my regret and strong desire to make it right make me squirm. I badly want to fix my transgression myself—to get a do-over. Instead, all that can be done is to lean on my husband's love and receive that which he is offering me. When I accept his forgiveness and put my failure as a wife behind me, he does the same. In this way, we experience restored relationship.

My husband's forgiveness serves as a model to help me better understand God's forgiveness and my response. Once we have confessed, grieved, and repented our sin, we must accept His grace lest our lives be hamstrung by self-condemnation. Time is passing away, and eternity is our imminent truth. So we must allow the future to shape our lives—not past failures!

We must be so humble and so consumed by the love of God that we receive His forgiveness willingly. We must humbly *forget what is behind and press on toward the goal to win the prize for which God has called us heavenward in Christ Jesus.*

And what is the prize toward which we are straining? It is this: *death will be swallowed up in victory, the mortal will be clothed with immortality, and our sins will be washed white as snow.* We will be found pure and holy because of what Jesus did, and even now, we find ourselves in this redeeming grace. This is our reality; we must live like it is true!

Embrace God's Word

For further insight, read Philippians 3:7-14; 1 Corinthians 15:54; Isaiah 1:18; and 1 John 1:8-9.

Journal Your Thoughts

Is there a past sin or failure you need to release to God so you can accept His forgiveness and press forward with abandon? Try to put into words that regret, and write a prayer of release to God.

Section Three

Apprehending Meaning

The Eternal Worth in Your Daily Living

And now these three remain: faith, hope and love. But the greatest of these is love.

—1 Corinthians 13:13

Clean the Toilet in Love

Do everything in love.
—1 Corinthians 16:14

*T*oday, I cleaned a toilet. Believe me, it needed to be done. My little ones had been using it regularly with varying rates of success, and that was starting to show. As I sprayed, wiped, and scrubbed, I began to reflect on this chore. I wondered what motivated me. I also wondered what I would *want* my motivation to be for such a task.

The answer to the latter question—and the former as well, I hope—is love. I want to love my parents well by pulling my weight with the cleaning. (They've taken us in while our house is being renovated.) I want to love my children well by providing them with a sanitary and soothing environment, and I believe a clean bathroom is part of that equation. I want to love my Savior well by *doing the tasks He has put before me wholeheartedly and unto Him*. And so, I clean.

This clean toilet will be dirtied again faster than I'd like to admit. My work will be frustrated. It will come undone. This reality is part of the curse we endure because of our sin. But God, in His great mercy, has made a way for us to overcome the emptiness of our decaying reality. Not only has He ushered us into new, eternal life through Jesus Christ but also He has supernaturally and mysteriously poured meaning back into our living. Even the most basic of tasks, when done in love, will endure, *while even the most spiritual or lofty of accomplishments will gain us nothing apart from love.*

At the end of the end, prophecy will cease, tongues will be stilled, and knowledge will pass away. In eternity, all the toilets we cleaned and nice things we did for others will be forgotten, but the love we exhibited, through even the most menial task or the most glorious act, will remain.

Do you want to make your moments ring into eternity? *Do everything in love.* There is nothing greater that God wants from us than to love Him, firstly, and secondly, to love our neighbor as ourselves: "And now these three remain: faith, hope and love. But the greatest of these is love" (1 Corinthians 13:13).

Embrace God's Word

For further insight, read Colossians 3:23-24 and 1 Corinthians 13:1-13.

Journal Your Thoughts

What have you been forgetting to do in love?

How would it change your outlook to serve others out of this overflow?

Love One Another

*You did not choose me, but I chose you and appointed you so that
you might go and bear fruit—fruit that will last—and so that
whatever you ask in my name the Father will give you. This is my
command: Love each other.*

—John 15:16-17

Since the early days of my walk with God, I have felt the weight of my
calling to share the gospel with those who do not know Jesus. The work of
evangelism is holy and urgent; we should be as deeply burdened for the lost-
ness of the world as God is.

As I have walked with God and learned more about what it means to
do life as a part of His body (the church), He has also opened my eyes to the
equally sacred and eternal importance of His people functioning as a body
by serving and loving one another as brothers and sisters in Christ. In fact,
it is through *our love for one another that the lost will know we are disciples of
Jesus.*

Within God's very nature there exists one God yet three distinct per-
sons (the Father, the Son, and the Holy Spirit), dwelling together in loving,
perfect relationship. His church is intended to exemplify *who He is.* That
calling is weightier than we know! We do this by devoting ourselves to one
another in brotherly, unified love. Many, many times throughout the Bible
we are urged to love one another. Within this wholehearted, God-birthed,
transcendent love for our brothers and sisters in Christ lies power to draw
thirsty souls to new life. It is deeply and divinely compelling.

We must remember that *Jesus is the Vine, and we are the branches*. When we allow God to work through us to plant and water seeds in the lives of those who do not know Him, we see glorious fruit produced in our midst. This fruit is not a product of the branch. Rather, the branch is a conduit for the work the Vine is already doing. In the same way, when we simply and wholly *love one another as fellow Christians, we also bear fruit that will last.* This, too, originates with the Vine. It is a holy and eternal offering to the Lord.

Let's recognize the gravity of our calling to one another, knowing that our love will give great glory to God and that it will endure.

Embrace God's Word

For further insight, read John 13:34-35; John 15:1-17; and 1 John 3:14-18.

Journal Your Thoughts

Is loving one another as Christian brothers and sisters a central priority in your life? If not, how could you begin to love in this radical way?

How have you been intentionally and specifically loved by a fellow Christian?

By Faith We Follow Him

And without faith it is impossible to please God, because anyone who comes to him must believe that he exists and that he rewards those who earnestly seek him.

—Hebrews 11:6

*F*aith is the *confident assurance that what we hope for will come to pass.* This confidence sets us free from the fear of death. It gives us the wisdom to live a holy life, the prudence to long for heaven, and the long-sightedness to patiently endure suffering.

When we have true, deep, wholehearted faith, it suddenly doesn't matter if we are not acclaimed in this world or if our life goes off plan. Just as early Christian believers *trusted God and were tortured, preferring to die rather than turn from God and be free,* we too must place our hope in the resurrection to a better life. When our faith is firmly planted in eternity, we learn to lay aside our self-centered agenda and walk out this life faithfully, come what may, knowing it is but a blip on the screen of eternity. When we are heavenly minded on this earth, it is to our credit.

By faith we wake up each morning and make a choice to walk in gratitude and joy, knowing that God is with us and that His grace will be sufficient for all our needs.

By faith we say no to things that may be fun for the moment but would ultimately pull us away from our Heavenly Father, knowing that there is exceedingly more to this life than momentary enjoyment.

By faith we love others with the same love Christ displayed when He washed the feet of His disciples, knowing that "no servant is greater than his Master" (John 13:16) and that *the greatest among us will be a servant to all.*

By faith we train up our children, diligently discipling and shepherding them to know and love the Lord as our ultimate priority for their lives. We set aside what is easiest in order to do what is best, knowing that we have been entrusted with these eternal souls and that no other goal compares with the privilege we have of spending our years with them continually leading them to Jesus.

By faith we honor and uphold the covenant of marriage. As wives, *we submit to our husbands as to the Lord*—not mindless obedience, but in a way that frees our husbands to rise up into the holy leadership role God is calling them into. We trust that God will bless our faithfulness to His way in methods beyond what we can comprehend. We believe that He has called us to exemplify the relationship between Christ and the church in our marriage, and we do our part with resolve.

By faith we receive God's love for us. We accept His grace and forgiveness, which are freely given to us, *forgetting what is behind and pressing on toward the goal.*

Our complete confidence in God is the very thing that enables us to live a radical life. We see and believe that He exists, that what He says is true, and that "He rewards those who earnestly seek Him" (Hebrews 11:6).

Embrace God's Word

For further insight, read Hebrews 11:1, 35-39; Matthew 23:11-12; Ephesians 5:22-33; and Philippians 3:13-14.

Journal Your Thoughts

What are you thinking about today as you consider faith?

How is your understanding of faith deepening?

A Mother's Call to Make Disciples

This is what the LORD says:

"Let not the wise boast of their wisdom
or the strong boast of their strength
or the rich boast of their riches,
but let the one who boasts boast about this:
that they have the understanding to know me,
that I am the LORD, who exercises kindness,
justice and righteousness on earth,
for in these I delight,"
declares the LORD.

—Jeremiah 9:23-24

*I*t is easy for us as parents to set our sights on the wrong goals for our children. We tend to emphasize good grades, education, athletics, and fine arts. Too often, our primary objective is to turn out successful and accomplished human beings who have the right degree and the right trophies in their trophy case. What we, as proud mothers, fail to realize in the midst of our parental ambition is that all these things will not matter in eternity. In and of themselves, they are nothing more than *loss when compared to the surpassing value of our children knowing Jesus.*

Before Christ's ascension to heaven, He gave a charge with His parting words: "go and make disciples" (Matthew 28:19). Unfortunately, in our twenty-first-century world, we do not fully comprehend the depth of that concept. Jesus's disciples followed Him, watching His every move and learning from Him in all situations for three years! This is a model for discipleship, and in this way the teacher demonstrates God's ways and applies His truth to varied situations. Over time, it is the ultimate equipping for life with God.

As mothers (and fathers), God has given us this same opportunity. Our children naturally live their lives alongside us. God has given us the privilege of fulfilling His command to make disciples right in our own homes. Therefore, we must be careful how we live, "making the most of every opportunity, because the days are evil" (Ephesians 5:16). We must, over all else, make it our primary parenting goal to help our children *know God*, follow His way, and view their lives in light of eternity.

Curricular and extracurricular activities are not bad things (especially when they are leveraged as a means to love others and to advance the kingdom of God). They can be a means by which we assign glory to God in our hearts as we work hard and exercise the gifts and abilities He gave us.

However, neither the wise, nor the strong, nor the rich will have anything to boast about in the presence of God. So, let us strive to instill in our children the things that *will* matter forever.

Embrace God's Word

For further insight, read Philippians 3:7; Matthew 28:19-20; John 17:3; and 1 Corinthians 1:18-31.

Journal Your Thoughts

What parenting goals do you have that are mostly worldly?

What parenting goals do you have that are mostly eternal?

How can you shift your focus to more eternal goals?

The Riches of Christ in Us

For,

> "Who has known the mind of the Lord
> so as to instruct him?"
> But we have the mind of Christ.
> —1 Corinthians 2:16

*W*e are too easily satisfied.

How often do we go about the business of life unaware of the depth and breadth of Christ's love for us? We settle for a few disjointed prayers throughout the day as our only means of connection with our Heavenly Father. We sell ourselves short of the *fullness of God*. When the love of God and the immeasurable treasure of His abiding presence in our lives are left inactivated throughout our moments and days, the loss is profound.

Do you know what you have in Christ? You have *His very mind*. The Spirit of the Eternal King lives in you. There is no limit to the love He has for you. The Lord longs to go with you into that difficult and strained relationship. He longs to go with you into the grocery shopping, homework help, and endless decision-making of motherhood. Each task and problem in our lives can be a holy offering to Him when done in recognition of, and thanks for, His love.

When we wash that sippy cup out of an overflow of God's love, we step further into our newness of life. We experience out-of-this-world joy, patience beyond our capacity, and lasting rewards.

When we practice and learn how to carry out *a ceaseless conversation with our Lord,* one in which we are not always actively talking, but we are always actively resting in His presence, bringing our thoughts before Him one by one, then we will begin to see how good and right and true and kind He really is.

God yearns to remind us of His love and to provide us with the grace we need for each situation if only we invite Him into our moments as we turn our hearts toward Him.

Allow His love to wash over you today, and discover what it means to enjoy the indescribable riches and power that are available to you as His follower. Live your eternal life today!

Embrace God's Word

For further insight, read Ephesians 3:17-19; 1 Thessalonians 5:16-18; and Ephesians 1:3.

Journal Your Thoughts

How would becoming more aware of Christ's presence in your days and His love for you change your life?

Take time to thank God for the riches He has made available to you today in Christ.

Knowing God

Now this is eternal life: that they know you, the only true God,
and Jesus Christ, whom you have sent.

—John 17:3

*G*rowing up in church, I knew a lot about God from a young age. I learned Bible stories and, as time went by, I even read much of the Bible for myself. I believed what I learned and read, and I committed my life to follow Jesus. I wanted to please Him. My ultimate objective in my spiritual life was to figure out how God wanted me to live and then do it.

After moving away to college, a mentor challenged me to read Scripture through a different lens. Rather than making it my mission to know about God, she encouraged me to seek to know Him personally—to dig into Scripture with the intent of ascertaining His unchanging character. I began to write a question at the top of my journal each day before I began reading: "Who are You, Lord?" As I prayed, read, and considered, I began to see how God's nature was being revealed in every verse and story across the whole Bible.

Because of this new perspective, I also began to better understand His character in the context of my own life. I experienced His faithfulness, provision, and love firsthand, and so my personal relationship with Him deepened. You see, God created us for relationship. He created us to know Him, and when we do, we are changed.

Jesus says *this is eternal life: that we may know the only true God, and Jesus Christ whom He has sent.* The pursuit of knowing God is holy. It is drenched in the eternal and transcends time and space. As we tap into God's abiding presence in our inner being, we learn what it means to *walk in step with Him in our everyday living.*

God has made himself known to us in many ways: *through what has been created, through the Holy Spirit,* through His precious written Word, and through His working in the midst of our own tangible, real experiences.

"The grass withers and the flowers fall, / but the word of our God endures forever" (Isaiah 40:8). Because God's Word is an eternal, breathtaking revelation of His nature, and because *the very essence of eternal life is to know God,* let us make it our mission to seek His face. Let us get to know Him personally by soaking in His Word and walking with Him through each day.

Embrace God's Word

For further insight, read Galatians 5:16; Romans 1:19-20; and John 16:13-15.

Journal Your Thoughts

Is the pursuit of knowing God (not just knowing about Him) a new way of thinking about your Christian faith?

How could you know Him more today?

Our Bodies, a Temple

*Do you not know that your bodies are temples of the Holy Spirit,
who is in you, whom you have received from God? You are not
your own; you were bought at a price. Therefore honor God with
your bodies.*

—1 Corinthians 6:19-20

*T*ake a moment to look down at your hands. Consider the body God has given you. What is the purpose of this flesh and blood, muscle and bone, eyes and smile with which you've been adorned? There are many answers, but I can give you a good summary: *it is for the glory of God.*

The design of the human body is complex and wonderful. It testifies to a genius and loving Creator. The way we interact with other people and our environment on this earth does likewise. Creation is an outflow of God's nature, and nothing exemplifies Him more than those He created in His image.

What's more, *the bodies of those who follow Christ are a temple of God Almighty.* Jesus purchased us at a high price with His own blood, which was poured out to ransom us from sin. Fitness, health, preening, and perceived beauty do not in any way greaten this holy truth. A prisoner for the faith in a persecuted nation who is sick, dirty, clothed in rags, and beaten down is as holy a vessel as one who is well-fed and glowing with health . . . and arguably even more so. A worn-out, unshowered, spit-up–clad mother is no less qualified as God's temple than a mother who is rested and perfectly put together.

Our bodies are to be given back to God every single day *as a living sacrifice.* When we feed and care for them, we diligently steward that with which we've been entrusted. When we dress them, may we do it to be an effective minister of God's grace in the cultural context in which God has placed us. We were created in Christ, not to get attention for ourselves, but simply "to do good works, which God prepared in advance for us to do" (Ephesians 2:10).

Above all else, as God's temple, we must not use our bodies for sin: "What fellowship can light have with darkness?" (2 Corinthians 6:14). Our bodies do not belong to ourselves. They are tools in God's hands to accomplish His will, and we must daily commit them to Him as such. *May Christ be exalted in our bodies, whether by life or by death,* whether in health or in sickness, and whether refreshed or exhausted. May it all be for His glory.

This sacrifice is holy and pleasing to God, our spiritual act of worship.

Embrace God's Word

For further insight, read Romans 12:1; Philippians 1:20; and 1 Corinthians 9:27.

Journal Your Thoughts

How do you see God's handiwork and genius in the body He has given you?

How can you practically offer it back to Him as a pleasing offering?

The Good Fruit of Suffering

*Not only so, but we also glory in our sufferings, because we know
that suffering produces perseverance; perseverance, character;
and character, hope.*

—Romans 5:3-4

*T*here is inherent suffering in motherhood. From the time that baby is conceived, we start to give of ourselves. Up to that point, our healthy young bodies were mostly unfamiliar with the feelings of protracted nausea, fatigue, insomnia, heartburn, swelling, hip pain, digestive discomfort, limited physical capacity, overwhelming emotions, and scarring stretch marks. We endure and wait patiently for the day when we will once again draw a satisfying and deep breath of fresh air. What more can we do? We try our best to enjoy those tiny kicks, our cute baby bump, and our new maternity clothes.

Bringing that sweet baby into the world is a process shrouded in pain, and recovering from childbirth is often a long and ginger process as well. At this point we learn that the giving has only just begun. Our sweet baby brings with him many life changes, needs, and limitations.

Because we love these little ones and yearn for them to be protected from all kinds of pain, we have a great vulnerability to even more personal suffering as they walk out their lives on this earth. When our children are hurt, rejected by peers, diagnosed with a disease, or taken from this life too soon, we walk a path of suffering that would not be possible apart from our motherhood. Though the joys are great, they do not erase the difficulties.

And yet, there is an unmistakable glory in all these sufferings. You see, *they produce the fruit of perseverance.* We learn what it means to trust God and keep showing up, even in the midst of the exhaustion, frustration, or uncertainty. *This perseverance, over time, produces character.* We become strong women who have weathered storms and been found faithful. As we journey with Christ, we discover within ourselves patience, resolve, and love for others that exceeds our self-love. And from this character, we obtain the great gem, melded together by the heat and compression of adversity: *hope.* This is exceedingly valuable!

This is not the "hope" of a pain-free life. No, this is the enduring hope of heaven. We learn what it means to lean into God's promises. And what are His promises? *Our sufferings will be wiped away. Evil will be vanquished. All things will be made new and right,* and in Christ we will go forth into eternal life. This hope is the thing that enables us to face life with grace and peace. Rather than dread suffering, we begin to discover what it means to embrace it, welcoming the good fruit it bears.

Embrace God's Word

For further insight, read Revelation 21:1-8; 1 Peter 5:10; and James 1:2-4.

Journal Your Thoughts

How have you experienced this metamorphosis from suffering to perseverance, to character, to hope in your own life?

Write a prayer giving God thanks for the good work He has done in your life through difficult things.

Created by Design

God blessed them and said to them, "Be fruitful and increase in
number; fill the earth and subdue it. Rule over the fish in the sea
and the birds in the sky and over every living creature that moves
on the ground."

—Genesis 1:28

When we do the very things that God created us to do, we bring glory to Him. Just as the blazing cosmos, the babbling brook, and the singing lark all cry out of God's goodness and might, so do we when we fulfill the roles for which He designed us.

When God created man and woman, He charged them to fill the earth and subdue it. When mankind busies itself with doing these two things, the genius of God, who is the Imaginer and Creator of all things, is magnified.

What does it mean to subdue the earth? Clearing land, farming, domesticating animals, and building roads, cities, and homes is all part of that process. So is the making of scientific discoveries. All of the hidden possibilities within this created realm began the moment God set the world in motion. As we explore art, design, music, and color, we bring to light the beauty, care, and creativity that God put in place. These things are good and honor the Lord as long as they do not oppose His character. Even those who do not know God will unknowingly bring Him glory as they function according to His design.

What does it mean to be fruitful and multiply? Having children is a part of this, certainly. God uses some women to multiply humanity according to His purposes. In our childbearing, God is exalted. Other women accept the invitation to multiply their lives into children through adoption and foster care. Even still, this multiplication and fruit-bearing concept goes far deeper. We multiply spiritual fruit as we allow God to take over our lives and flow through us. The Holy Spirit in us will produce many good fruits in our lives including *love, joy, peace, patience, kindness, goodness, faithfulness, gentleness, and self-control* (see Galatians 5:22-23). By His working, He will also give us spiritual children as we plant and water seeds in the lives of others—those we have the privilege of discipling for the sake of the kingdom of heaven. We do this simply by sharing gospel hope, expressing God's love in tangible ways, and teaching others to obey His commands.

Today, as you fulfill your God-given and honored role in this grand and glorious drama, be conscious of how it is working together according to His design. Worship God for His marvelous creation, and take heart as you "do your thing" with the purpose and joy of one who is exalting the Lord.

Embrace God's Word

For further insight, read Psalm 139:13-18; Psalm 19:1; Job 12:7-10; and John 15:5.

Journal Your Thoughts

God designed women to be and do certain things for His glory. He has also given each of us specific gifts and passions. Write ways you can glorify God simply by living out His design for *you*.

Laying Aside What I Think I Deserve

Command them to do good, to be rich in good deeds, and to be generous and willing to share. In this way they will lay up treasure for themselves as a firm foundation for the coming age, so that they may take hold of the life that is truly life.

—1 Timothy 6:18-19

I have reached countless breaking points since becoming a mother, all of which ultimately paved the way for unprecedented spiritual growth and depth with God. After years of wrestling, God graciously brought me to the point of surrendering things like comfort, outside assistance, control, sleep, breaks, entertainment, pampering, "me time," goals, date nights, and personal pursuits.

There is freedom in surrender. As we let go of our plans, entitlements, and ideas of what life should be, we offer our lives to Jesus on a new level—not just on a big-picture scale but also on a today, in-this-moment sort of way.

Through this process of surrender, we learn what it means to function out of God's strength rather than our own—to walk in step with Him and to follow Him in each moment. This new rhythm replaces our former tendency to demand our rights or to fixate on our own happiness or ease of living.

This new attitude of surrender has had challenging implications in my life:

- It means *guarding my mouth from complaining.*
- It means staying open to things that God might call me to do.
- It means choosing joy and gratitude every day.
- It means letting go of control and *trusting God with outcomes.*
- It means surrendering my plans with open hands.

The purpose of our lives is not comfort or diversion. Truly, this life is a mist in the wind. How wrongly we often gauge its value, due to our folly! We pursue all the wrong things when we spend our brief moments on the earth consumed with ourselves and pursuing present rewards rather than *laying up treasures in heaven* in faith through obedient, surrendered, eternity-minded lives.

When we are willing to follow God unreservedly, we get to experience the unparalleled blessings of His provision and favor both now and eternally. And if that means this life does not look like what we think we deserve, that is far more okay than we may realize.

When we reach the end of ourselves, we find the glorious free fall of trust. This is where the adventure is found. This is the life lived abundantly! It is truly rich.

Embrace God's Word

For further insight, read Philippians 2:12-16; Proverbs 3:5-6; and Galatians 2:20.

Journal Your Thoughts

Is there a point of struggle in your life today where you are not getting all you feel you deserve?

Write a prayer to God surrendering your entitlement and taking up His mission.

Gold, Silver, and Precious Stones

If anyone builds on this foundation [Jesus Christ] using gold, sil-
ver, costly stones, wood, hay, or straw, their work will be shown for
what it is, because the Day will bring it to light. It will be revealed
with fire, and the fire will test the quality of each person's work. If
what has been built survives, the builder will receive a reward. If
it is burned up, the builder will suffer loss but yet will be saved—
even though only as one escaping through the flames.

—1 Corinthians 3:12-15

*T*hose of us who are in Christ share the same foundation, which is, of
course, Jesus. On the day of judgment, these lives of ours will be tested by
fire, and we can know with confidence that our foundation will withstand.
It is not based on what we do, but on who He is and what He has done for us!
When we *receive Him,* this foundation is laid *by grace through faith,* and it will
endure on that day.

However, the rest of our lives, or the metaphorical houses we are building on top of that foundation, will also be tested by fire. In these verses, we
see that we can be in Christ (having the right foundation) and yet fail to have
anything else worthwhile to show for our lives in eternity.

The question will be, did we build with worldly commodities—the
wood, hay, and straw, which represent a self-focused and worldly empire? Or
did we build with the precious, enduring stones of obedience, trust in God
for future reward, humble and quiet service to others, and the laying down
of our lives daily that we might bring about God's will? This is the building
that will last.

When we are confident that we will receive a future reward, our way of living changes. We accept sacrifice because we are looking ahead to what will come.

When we defer pleasure or personal gain in this life for the sake of the kingdom, our faith is proven true in multiple realms. God is glorified *before a great cloud of witnesses (the faithful who have gone before us)*, in the presence of heavenly beings, and in the lives of Christ followers who are bolstered in their faith.

May we not be women just barely escaping through flames on the day of judgment, surrounded by the disintegrating remnants of our worldly ambition, self-interest, and vanity. Let us wisely choose to live God's way with our whole will and being.

Embrace God's Word

For further insight, read John 1:12; Ephesians 2:8-9; Hebrews 12:1; Matthew 25:23; and Hebrews 11:6.

Journal Your Thoughts

What pursuits in your life is God showing you that are wood, hay, and straw?

What about those that are gold, silver, and precious stones?

Spend time praying and asking Him to open your eyes to see how you are building.

The Word of God Endures Forever

As the Scriptures say,

"People are like grass;
  their beauty is like a flower in the field.
The grass withers and the flower fades.
  But the word of the Lord remains forever."

And that word is the Good News that was preached to you.

—1 Peter 1:24-25 (NLT)

*W*hen people and grass have long since faded away, the Word of the Lord will remain.

Does that mean that, at the end of time when the earth is gone, a pile of Bibles will be all that's left? No, the Word of God is so much more than paper and ink! It is the revelation of God to us. The Holy Scriptures, Jesus, and the gospel message are "the Word." The Word is the story of what God has done, the blazing light of His glory and love as revealed to us, and the embodiment of His goodness and might. It is too holy and precious for words, and yet, it is the stuff of words—living words.

"The word of God is alive and active. Sharper than any double-edged sword, it penetrates even to dividing soul and spirit, joints and marrow; it judges the thoughts and attitudes of the heart" (Hebrews 4:12). God's Word has the power to give life or to condemn us. It holds sway over all creation, and it is a precious treasure indeed.

In Christ, we have been given new life, and this new life will last forever; this new life *has come from and through the eternal, living Word of God.* The life our earthly parents gave us will end in death, but that is not where our story ends. Now, through the hope of the good news, we live with the wonderful expectation of what is to come—a priceless inheritance that has been reserved for us as God's children.

Today, in the midst of our wildflower life, we have the opportunity to glory in the light of eternity simply by abiding in and obeying God's Word. We do this by loving our Christian brothers and sisters, rejecting sin, trusting God in the midst of trials, exercising self-control, and being holy even as God himself is holy. When we make it our mission to obey God's Word, our life will be characterized by the eternal. And thus, the glorious, inexpressible joy of that hope is ours.

Embrace God's Word

For further insight, read 1 Peter 1:3-25 and John 14:15.

Journal Your Thoughts

How have you experienced the power of God's eternal, living Word in your own life?

What is one way you will resolve to know and obey God's Word today?

Poured-Out Mother

But even if I am being poured out like a drink offering on the
sacrifice and service coming from your faith, I am glad and
rejoice with all of you.

—Philippians 2:17

Sarah has several young children, including an infant, just like me. After a rough winter filled with sickness, loneliness, and multiple little trials all adding up together in a big way (not to mention hormones and sleep deprivation), she is struggling. Sarah feels that joy is elusive, and she is left weary and longing for heaven. Ever been there? Me too.

By the end of each day, she is emptied. And so, she asks God to receive her poured-out life as an offering to Him, recognizing that He has entrusted her with this work for His glory.

That feeling of being poured out to the last drop is the reality of many mothers. The exhaustion is overwhelming at times. Through this example of stubborn faithfulness to glorify God in the midst of difficult days, we learn to envision motherhood as an offering. Just as in ancient times, a priest poured out a drink offering on the alter in the temple of the Lord, so we do this with our very lives. We learn and embrace what it means to walk forward in obedience and trust. As we put into practice the things we believe about God, persevering day by day, *then will we become* "mature and complete, not lacking anything" (James 1:4).

And so, we must surrender our expectations about life and, instead, walk in step with His Spirit. We must live His truths in the midst of the life He has assigned to us regardless of how it compares to the lives of those around us. *We must allow Him to be strong through our weakness and learn what it means to rely on His grace.* By this simple but essential positioning of our heart, all our working, struggling, and exhaustion become eternally significant.

All that truly matters in this life is that we live the moments faithfully and obediently. Our days are numbered, and that number is a mystery. May we turn to God in the midst of the hardest days of our mothering, and may we learn what it means to walk in grace and trust, welcoming eternity into our daily trials.

Embrace God's Word

For further insight, read 2 Corinthians 12:9; 1 John 3:16; and Romans 12:1-2.

Journal Your Thoughts

Do you resist the assignment God has given you today as too demanding, or do you embrace it as your offering to Him?

Write a prayer asking God to help you in times of trouble—when life is overwhelming.

Spiritually Minded Relationships

This is how God showed his love among us: He sent his one and only Son into the world that we might live through him. ... Dear friends, since God so loved us, we also ought to love one another. No one has ever seen God; but if we love one another, God lives in us and his love is made complete in us.

—1 John 4:9, 11-12

*M*any times, I have been guilty of taking relationships and human interactions at face value. Be it that business client, the young mom at church, the mailman, my parents, that neighbor, or my child's friend, it is easy and tempting to focus on what they can do for me or what I want from them. I naturally focus on my own insecurities and how the other person negatively or positively affects my day-to-day life. Yet these momentary and self-centered inclinations are ultimately unimportant and incorrect.

Each of these people is not just flesh and blood, words and actions; he or she is an eternal being. Each of them is passionately and jealously loved by the God who made the ultimate sacrifice for him or her. Each person is walking out a spiritual journey, and the condition of each heart is God's chief concern. *Our Father is always at work; He longs for everyone to be saved.* If a person does not know Him, God is working to bring him or her to salvation. If a person has already received and experienced new life, God is working to make him or her more like Christ. God's perspective and goals for people are always spiritually rooted.

As children of God, we are His agents. Our hearts should burn just as His does. We must always be aware of God's desires for the lives of those around us. We must put these truths above our own self-interests.

This paradigm changes our work relationships, our marriage, our mothering, our conversations with our parents, and our dealings with all customer service representatives everywhere who are not telling us what we want to hear. When we take on a spiritual mind-set, we will give ourselves over to Jesus and allow Him to work though us to express and accomplish His enduring will. His love will be manifest, His truth proclaimed, and the kingdom of God advanced in lives around us.

So, next time we see that young mom at church or our neighbor out in her yard, let us look at her as God sees her. Let us choose to recognize the relevance of eternity in her life and make ourselves available to minister to her as the Holy Spirit leads. This might mean offering a warm smile or choosing to listen instead of talk. May we discover what it means to live spiritually minded relationships in light of eternity.

Embrace God's Word

For further insight, read John 5:17; 1 Timothy 2:3-4; and Philippians 2:3-4.

Journal Your Thoughts

What would it mean for you to approach your relationships from a spiritual, eternal, kingdom-minded perspective?

How would this influence your response to a difficult person?

The Eternal Significance of Mothering

These commandments that I give you today are to be on your hearts. Impress them on your children. Talk about them when you sit at home and when you walk along the road, when you lie down and when you get up.

—Deuteronomy 6:6-7

After God created man and woman in His own image, He blessed them both. Then, He instructed them to *be fruitful and multiply, to fill the earth and subdue it.* And so, "Adam named his wife Eve, because she would become the mother of all the living" (Genesis 3:20). From the beginning, our mothering design was woven into the very essence of who God made us to be.

Although we know that our family unit will not look the same in eternity, there is still great eternal significance in our mothering, should we choose to find and embrace it.

As mothers, we play a role in the fulfillment of God's plan for His creation. When we bear, nurture, and guide children, and when we discipline and instruct them in love, we are glorifying the Creator who brilliantly imagined and fashioned family to satisfy these functions. When we teach our children who God is and what it means to follow Him in the context of our home, the kingdom of God moves forward.

The children we mother are eternal beings. They have been entrusted to us by the Maker of all things, and they are unimaginably precious to Him. The importance of advancing our career, monetary gain, and ease of living diminish greatly when compared with the surpassing charge and responsibility we have to usher these little ones to the foot of the cross. We *make disciples* right in our own homes as God leads. Their salvation is God's work, not ours, but we have the incredible privilege of participating in His work in their lives as we pray and as we help them connect what they see, know, and experience with spiritual truth.

Heavenly minded mothering is a sacred calling. We must not become distracted and encumbered by the world's views of what this role should look like. Instead, we must take time to carefully seek God and listen to His desires for us and our children. We must *fix our eyes on Jesus and run this race well* with God's agenda for our families as our chief and only concern.

Embrace God's Word

For further insight, read Genesis 1:27-28; Matthew 28:16-20; and Hebrews 12:1-2.

Journal Your Thoughts

Take time to thank God for the sacred, purposeful responsibility of motherhood, and ask Him to give you wisdom for this task.

Redeeming Vacations

*Command those who are rich in this present world not to be
arrogant nor to put their hope in wealth, which is so uncertain,
but to put their hope in God, who richly provides us with everything for our enjoyment.*

—1 Timothy 6:17

*T*his year, my extended family and I went on a Caribbean cruise together.
In the midst of so much extravagance and beauty, I found needed space to
think and pray and study and ponder. In fact, as I write this, I sit on a wide
deck surrounded by ocean on every side. It led me to consider the value of
a vacation.

Not long ago, I had the privilege of hearing my friend Joe share his story.
Joe's journey out of darkness and into new life with Christ started on a plane
to Jamaica. A friendly man with a big personality was seated across the aisle.
This man was a Christian who shared the gospel with my friend on that
flight, and as a result, over the course of the following weeks, God brought
about Joe's salvation. His life was radically changed.

That man on the plane? It turns out, he was a pastor on vacation.

Futility is found when we believe that our vacations are solely about us.
It is found when we check out of life and put on the mind-set of self-service.

However, vacations are redeemed when we go with God. They are
redeemed when we focus on the mission of His kingdom each day by notic-
ing and intentionally loving all those with whom we come into contact.
Vacations are redeemed when we leverage them as a time of intentional rest,
recharging, relaxing, and deeply communing with our Heavenly Father.

They are redeemed when we take them as a holy opportunity to cultivate and further invest in deep and life-giving relationships with family and friends. They are redeemed when we glorify God for the vastness and beauty of the places we visit. And finally, vacations are redeemed when we lay down our will to offer them solidly back to God.

So, before you plan to spend hundreds or thousands of dollars on your next vacation, consider whether or not God wants you to sacrifice luxury so you may show generosity to a brother or sister in Christ who is in need. If so, you can rejoice, knowing that you were obedient! If you feel released to go on your vacation, go with God, go in joy, and go in surrender, giving each day of your trip back to Him. Make your plans secondary to the work He may want to do in the lives around you, and be sure to give Him the thanks and glory!

Embrace God's Word

For further insight, read Matthew 6:33; Ephesians 5:15-20; and 1 Timothy 6:17-19.

Journal Your Thoughts

How can you live radically even in the context of vacation?

Do you have a trip coming up? Spend time offering it back to God in whatever way He chooses.

Redeeming Home

*She watches over the affairs of her household
and does not eat the bread of idleness.
Her children arise and call her blessed;
her husband also, and he praises her.*

—Proverbs 31:27-28

I believe that, as women, we have a natural bent toward homemaking somewhere in us. Whether we work outside the home, whether we are married, whether we have children, or whether we are good at homemaking, we possess an inherent, God-given, nurturing nature that stirs us to cultivate home in various ways. This is good!

And yet our physical homes have an expiration date. The tidying and dusting will all come undone, and the money and effort we spend to build, buy, remodel, decorate, or situate our home is ultimately all for naught. Not to mention all that cleaning! All these things are passing away and will soon be forgotten. In and of themselves, even our homes are meaningless. But yet, through Christ, eternity seeps into every area of our working and living.

Because of what Christ has done, we draw meaning from our work simply by offering it as a pleasing sacrifice to the Lord. *When we work heartily at the roles in which we find ourselves for His glory, we store up an inheritance in eternity.* What a gift to have such rich meaning infused into our simple, daily toil.

What's more, when we offer our home back to God to use as He wills, when we let go of our entitlements and swing open the door to welcome others in, and when we show love-rooted hospitality to our brothers and sisters in Christ, our earthly homes take on significance in the kingdom of heaven. They become a tool for God to use in powerful ways to show the world who He is.

Therefore, let us "make" our homes in response to our God-given charge to bless, serve, and care well for our families. Let us complete this task diligently for God's glory. Let us understand that a home is not defined by how immaculately kept or extravagantly decorated and furnished it is. May we instead create a space for others to experience Christ's love through hospitality within our home.

If this is truly our heart's bent, we can know that our homemaking truly matters.

Embrace God's Word

For further insight, read Colossians 3:23-24; Titus 2:3-5; and Proverbs 31:10-31.

Journal Your Thoughts

Do you show hospitality readily? If not, what holds you back?

How could you bring God into your homemaking efforts all the more?

Redeeming a Good Life

For the LORD God is a sun and shield;
the LORD bestows favor and honor;
no good thing does he withhold
from those whose walk is blameless.
—Psalm 84:11

A good life is a gift from God. Protection, met needs, and abundance are provisions from Him. He loves to bless His faithful ones, and He lavishes love on those who trust in Him: "His mercy extends to those who fear Him, / from generation to generation" (Luke 1:50); "He has filled the hungry with good things" (v. 53). Just as we glorify God in the midst of suffering through patient perseverance and trust, so also, we glorify Him in the midst of good days through grateful hearts and praise. In both of these times, eternity and earth collide, and the Lord is held up in honor.

Perhaps you look at your own life today and marvel at the good things God has given you. Perhaps your physical needs are fulfilled, you live in safety, your husband loves you well, and your children are a delight to you. If you have everything you need and so much more, may you recognize that all this is from the hand of God. For His own good reasons, God has chosen to lavish His provision on you in this way. This is an overflow of His goodness, and He is worthy of all the thanks and praise! With great faithfulness, He has given you your daily bread in the form of food, clothing, shelter, and community.

In the same breath, if you find yourself in a season of loss, heartache, or waiting, take heart and be reminded that God is still faithful, and loves you as deeply as the one in a season of abundance. His mercy is at work in your life as well, although you cannot know the full picture of what He is doing on this side of heaven.

Giving good gifts to His children is a way in which God brings glory to Himself. We have an essential role to play as recipients of His mercy, simply in deflecting all glory to Him, boasting in His goodness alone, acknowledging that all these things are from God, and placing our trust in Him rather than in the hope of a pain-free or perfect life. Let us fill our hearts and mouths with thanksgiving in the midst of good days, but may we not put our hope in them. Let us learn to be content and grateful in all things and to appreciate the goodness of God, however it manifests itself in our lives today.

May we receive from God with open hands and walk in obedience to Him, trusting that He sees the eternal picture and that He is working everything together for the good of those who love Him, regardless of the circumstances we see.

Embrace God's Word

For further insight, read Micah 6:8; Romans 8:28; and John 21:20-23.

Journal Your Thoughts

What good things has God provided you with today? Take time to thank Him.

Are you walking through painful trials? Thank Him.

Redeeming Influence and Position

Brothers and sisters, each person, as responsible to God, should remain in the situation they were in when God called them.
— 1 Corinthians 7:24

*I*nfluence and fame in this world are fleeting. Like a bottomless bucket, they hold no water or merit in eternity, nor can they save anyone from the coming judgment. Those who jockey for power and recognition at the expense of other people, their personal integrity, or more lasting pursuits make a sorry trade. To run after position in this world is to give it up in heaven, for *the least on earth shall be the greatest in heaven, and the last on earth shall be first in heaven.* In fact, "anyone who wants to be first must be the very last, and the servant to all," just as Christ demonstrated (Mark 9:35).

But what about those believers who, for one reason or another, do find themselves in positions of influence? God is strategic and wise! Although to pursue these things for worldly gain is to chase the wind, God will use a surrendered life to accomplish His purposes on every scale. Through Scripture we see that at times God places His people in positions of power to accomplish His will for His glory.

So, in whatever situation we find ourselves when we become believers, we should be ready to stay right there! Or, as we sense the Holy Spirit leading us, we should be prepared to step forward into positions of influence in faith, knowing that God can do anything and that it is He who is at work. As we allow God to use us according to His plan, we must always remember that

He purchased us at a high price, so we must not be enslaved by the world. We must remember that *the proud will be humbled but the humble will be honored,* and so, even in the midst of position, we must clothe ourselves in humility, kindness, and love. We must give Him the glory.

Even Paul, who was well spoken, well trained, scholarly, influential, and powerful in his own right, did not boast in his knowledge or wisdom. Rather, he threw himself on the power of Christ and boasted only in the foolishness of the gospel, which is the power of God for all who believe. For God makes the wisdom of the world to be foolishness, and "God chose the foolish things of the world to shame the wise" (1 Corinthians 1:27). To God alone belongs the praise.

Embrace God's Word

For further insight, read Luke 22:24-30; 1 Corinthians 7:17-24; Luke 14:11; and 1 Corinthians 1:26-31.

Journal Your Thoughts

What areas of influence or position have you been entrusted with?

How will you leverage the influence God has given you for His glory?

Redeeming Fashion

I also want the women to dress modestly, with decency and pro-
priety, adorning themselves, not with elaborate hairstyles or gold
or pearls or expensive clothes, but with good deeds, appropriate
for women who profess to worship God.

—1 Timothy 2:9-10

*F*ashion and appearances are so, so temporary. Yet there is freedom here—and even a glimmer of eternity—should we leverage these correctly and should our hearts be pure before the Lord.

As Christian women, we are called to be modest, and true modesty lends itself to an element of care. It is a deep, rich, God-honoring concept. In fact, Christian women are exhorted to be modest in three ways. *First, we must not draw attention to ourselves with flashy accessories or attire. Second, we must do good. Third, we must choose decent and appropriate clothing* as we are able.

What's more, we see that the Proverbs 31 woman is dignified and beautiful, a source of purity and light in a dark world as well as a source of honor to her husband: "She is clothed in fine linen and purple. / Her husband is respected at the city gate" (Proverbs 31:22-23).

These examples demonstrate that, by presenting ourselves well, we are able to honor God. The essence of order, beauty, self-discipline, and dignity all trace back to our Heavenly Father. We must deflect attention wholeheartedly to Him—not finding within our appearance an erroneous source of worth, but instead seeking to be our best selves for His glory. And thus, we must craft our wardrobe and care for our bodies only as much as they make us effective for the kingdom of God within the context God has placed us.

We must not consume our time with appearances, but we can leverage these to minister effectively to the culture around us. Our beauty must come from the good things we do and the outflow of God's love in us. That love is not concerned with self; it is consumed with the best interests of our neighbor. May we never intentionally or carelessly lead another believer to jealousy or envy, but may we instead present ourselves only as nicely as it benefits those around us, giving us favor to influence their lives for Jesus. Just as Paul became all things to all people, so might God call us to adjust our fashion to the culture around us.

Let us be modest—not just in clothing, but in heart. And let us be wise in all things. Let us be good stewards of the resources God has given us, not lavishing on ourselves, but appropriately allocating resources. May we not be consumed by the things of the world, *but may we hold them loosely, as though not engrossed in them.* Let us wear clothes that glorify our Lord, not ourselves, and may we have fun, knowing that God is the Source of color and design and creativity.

Let us be disciplined and effective as women of God, *seeking first the kingdom of God in all things.*

Embrace God's Word

For further insight, read 1 Corinthians 7:29-31 and Matthew 6:33.

Journal Your Thoughts

Do you dress to draw attention to yourself or to deflect it wholly to God?

How can you commit even your appearance to the Lord?

Treasures in Heaven: Laboring for God

The one who plants and the one who waters have one purpose,
and they will each be rewarded according to their own labor.
—1 Corinthians 3:8

*I*n this world, we are surrounded by people hungering to know God. They are lost, spiritually blind, and dead in sin, and yet God has planted eternity in their hearts. The ache and longing is real for all people, no matter how deeply they may have stifled it or how vehemently they may have numbed it.

Despite this mutual, innate spiritual inclination, there is a temptation for those of us who know the truth to refrain from broaching spiritual topics because we feel embarrassed or insecure in what others will think of us. This has been an inner battle for me throughout my life.

And yet great and unspeakable blessings come to those who possess the perspective to labor in the fields of the Lord. When our lives on this earth are compared to eternity, it is unthinkable that we let something so trivial as fear of man or concern for our image stand in the way of the work God wants to do in the lives around us. This is why we must surrender our story to God to use as He wishes. It is why *we must be prepared to give an answer for the hope we have* as the Spirit of God prompts us, and why we offer *petitions, prayers, intercessions, and thanksgiving for all people.*

When we see the brevity of our world and the greatness of God, we will have the power to lay aside our own insecurities and walk in obedience *knowing that we will be rewarded according to our labor, and knowing that God wants to save sinners like us from death through the power of the gospel.* This matters immensely! The angels in heaven rejoice when one sinner repents and finds life.

When we allow God to deeply open our eyes to eternal realities, we will be so consumed with love for others and concern with their eternal destination that we will plant and water seeds of truth at every opportunity, disregarding our precious reputation. As we see our own desperation for God more clearly, we will have a similar desperation that others know and experience the same gift of His salvation, which has transformed us.

May we make the most of every opportunity, for the days are evil. May we be known as a God-clinger, love-giver, and hope-sharer, and may we discover what it means to *crucify self* and embrace the mission of the kingdom.

Embrace God's Word

For further insight, read 1 Peter 3:15; 1 Timothy 2:1-6; Ephesians 5:15-20; Galatians 2:20; and James 5:20.

Journal Your Thoughts

Is there someone in your life to whom God is prompting you to speak about Him?

What steps can you take to share the good news of Jesus?

Treasures in Heaven: Sacrificing for the Sake of the Gospel

"Truly I tell you," Jesus replied, "no one who has left home or brothers or sisters or mother or father or children or fields for me and the gospel will fail to receive a hundred times as much in this present age: homes, brothers, sisters, mothers, children and fields—along with persecutions—and in the age to come eternal life."

—Mark 10:29-30

*S*acrifice is a difficult thing. It is painful. It is generally not much fun.

And yet God, in His wisdom, chose sacrifice to be the means through which heaven and earth would be reconciled. Jesus—Emmanuel—left His glory to enter into a world of sin and pain. God the Father gave His only Son to die for our sins. In response, we lay down our lives to follow Him. We sacrifice in response to His sacrifice because we believe and know that He loves us and that what He says is true, so this ultimately is not difficult. Sacrifice is the catalyst for redemption.

There is great glory and beauty and power here. You see, sacrifice flows from love. In its very nature, it is a voluntary action. As love compels us, we give something up for the benefit of another.

As mothers, we live this out in small ways every day. With God's help, we do not hesitate to sacrifice for our children; whether they are hungry, thirsty, cold, or lonely, we would rather personally do without than see them lack. In this way, we bear God's image: "Greater love has no one than this: to lay down one's life for one's friends" (John 15:13). Sacrifice is the ultimate litmus test for love, and thus, it is the definition of love: "This is how we know what love is: Jesus Christ laid down his life for us. And we ought to lay down our lives for our brothers and sisters" (1 John 3:16).

When we make sacrifices for the sake of the gospel, we put our actions where our faith is. We demonstrate our love for God, and He gets the glory. *What matters in this world is faith expressing itself in love.* For this reason, our sacrifices result in eternal rewards. Everything we leave and give up in order to follow Jesus, because we love Him, *will be returned to us a hundredfold* both now and *in the age to come.* When we believe this, we will have the strength and courage to give everything to God and live eternity today.

Embrace God's Word

For further insight, read Galatians 5:6; Philippians 2:4-8; and John 3:16.

Journal Your Thoughts

How has God given you an opportunity to sacrifice for Him?

Thank Him, knowing you will receive a hundred times as much in this age and in the age to come.

Treasures in Heaven: Withstanding Trials and Persecution

Blessed are you when people insult you, persecute you and falsely say all kinds of evil against you because of me. Rejoice and be glad, because great is your reward in heaven, for in the same way they persecuted the prophets who were before you.

—Matthew 5:11-12

I used to be very fearful of the prospect and reality of persecution as a Christ follower. I was so sensitive to this fear that I could not even read the stories about the plight of Christians around the globe. I prayed some, but mostly, I tried not to think about it. I was very disturbed and alarmed. Even though I personally lived in peace, I recognized that things could change or that God could call me to go to a dangerous part of the world. I struggled greatly with the suffering other Christians were enduring even though I was not directly affected.

In a sense, this sentiment of mutual grief is good. As Christians, we are one global body because we are one in Him, and just as in a body, "if one part suffers, every part suffers with it" (1 Corinthians 12:26).

However, as my faith has grown, I've learned to see persecution from an eternal viewpoint. Let me ask you, who is truly blessed?

Is it the one who lives an easy, smooth, comfortable life in this world but who never knows the power of God to break free from sin and self-interest?

Or is it the one who suffers in this life and thus becomes strong in faith in such a way that she *is done with sin,* so that she sets her heart on heaven, and so that she amasses eternal treasures as a result of her patient endurance?

This is the kind of question I ask myself, and when the scope of eternity is taken into consideration, it is clear to see that *those who have suffered and persevered are blessed.* Those who have suffered know what it means to have hope rooted in heaven, to experience all-in faith, and to follow God to places of trust and surrender they could not know otherwise. Oftentimes, they are also the ones who experience God's miraculous provision and see the kingdom of God move forward most.

As my perspective has shifted, I've become passionate about following the stories of persecuted Christians around the world. I allow these stories to drive me to prayer. I fervently pray for Christ's kingdom to come on the earth, and for Him to return and bring an end to this suffering. I ask God for miraculous provision for Christians facing persecution, and it is exciting to hear stories of how He is answering those prayers! But I also pray that God would give those affected (and me) the faith to suffer and die for Him. There is a blessing here, and it is one that will endure infinitely long past the pain.

Embrace God's Word

For further insight, read 1 Peter 4:1-2; James 5:10-11; James 1:12; and 1 Peter 1:3-9.

Journal Your Thoughts

How does eternity affect your view of trials and persecution?

Write a prayer asking God to pour out faith, protection, comfort, and strength into the lives of those who are facing persecution right now across the globe.

Treasures in Heaven: Quiet Deeds of Faith

But when you pray, go into your room, close the door and pray to your Father, who is unseen. Then your Father, who sees what is done in secret, will reward you.

—Matthew 6:6

Our world is loud, and our nature as humans is to want attention and honor for ourselves. We have a broken need to prove our worth and a sinful compulsion to glorify ourselves. So many people, in so many ways, are standing up and saying, "Look at me!" Maybe that's not you, but maybe it is on some level. And when this type of bragging, whether subtle or overt, is about spiritual matters, it especially does not sit well. Self-glorifying is not fitting for those who follow Christ.

In fact, we are called to do quite the opposite. We are called to practice deeds of faith in secrecy. To do this requires one thing: faith. If we go into a closet to pray, if we commit to a time of fasting, if we give to those in need, but no one ever knows of our diligence and sacrifice, we run the risk of receiving no benefit. No one will be impressed. No one will honor us. No one will be encouraged to do likewise. No one will hear the advice woven into our prayer and put it into action. However, through these private acts, we demonstrate that we believe God. We show that we expect our prayers, fasting, and giving to have an effect on the kingdom of God simply because He hears us, sees us, and answers us—not because we have done something in our own strength. In this way, we cultivate an intimate relationship with our Heavenly Father and prove that we trust Him and know *that He will reward us,* just as He said He would.

In this way, *we exercise self-control* because, after all, it is not always easy to keep these otherwise impressive matters secret. But with practice and diligence, quiet deeds of faith become beautiful, intimate, enduring, eternal gems known only to us and our Heavenly Father.

We relinquish the praise of people so God may be glorified. And God delights to give these things back to us, not just in this broken world, but in heaven forever. So, press on, and practice quiet deeds in faith!

Embrace God's Word

For further insight, read Matthew 6:1-6; Matthew 6:16-18; and Proverbs 25:28.

Journal Your Thoughts

How are you at keeping deeds of faith in your life private, even when you know others might be impressed?

Write a prayer asking God to grow your faith in future rewards and to show you how to practically apply the concept of trust through secrecy.

Treasures in Heaven: Doing Good

For we must all appear before the judgment seat of Christ, so that each of us may receive what is due us for the things done while in the body, whether good or bad.

—2 Corinthians 5:10

There exists an important relationship between good works and salvation. We know we cannot earn salvation through our good works. God is holy, and *our righteousness is like filth when compared to Him. It is by grace alone, through faith, that we are pulled from death and into eternal life.* Praise be to God!

But of course, real, alive faith will always produce fruit. *A lack of fruit invariably reveals not just a weak faith, but a dead faith.* And here is the test: do we obey God, and do we love other Christians—not just in theory, but in practice? When we truly love God and belong to Him, we will both believe Him and care about the things He cares about.

God will reward us for the love we show through good works. *If we give even a cup of water in Jesus's name to someone because he belongs to the Messiah, we will certainly not lose our reward.* In our society, water is nearly free. If something as simple as this will ring out into eternity, imagine how much more reward will result from greater sacrifices birthed out of genuine love for one another?

"For we must all appear before the judgment seat of Christ, so that each of us may receive what is due us for the things done while in the body, whether good or bad" (2 Corinthians 5:10). Jesus will want to know whether we cared for Him or overlooked Him on this earth. And indeed, whatever we have done for the least of these brothers and sisters of His, we have done for Him.

Good works cannot save us, but they are the sight glass of our faith. They cannot save us, but we will be judged according to them. Good works matter eternally.

So, give water. Share food. Meet needs. Extend friendship. Listen openly. Love well. Speak truth. Offer hope. And do good. In this way, *you will have treasures in heaven.*

Embrace God's Word

For further insight, read Isaiah 64:6; Ephesians 2:8-9; James 2:20-26; 1 John 4:20-21; Mark 9:41; and Matthew 25:31-46.

Journal Your Thoughts

In what ways have you tangibly loved a Christian brother or sister lately or helped someone in need?

How can you practically "do good" this week?

Glorify the Lord

But God made the earth by his power;
he founded the world by his wisdom
and stretched out the heavens by his
understanding.

—Jeremiah 10:12

*G*od created the world.

He imagined the earth and masterminded the laws that govern our universe. He is the one who set into motion every innate possibility that we now explore and enjoy. He also breathed ability, wisdom, and creativity into us, fashioning us in His very own image. Every discovery and technological or scientific advancement is but the tip of the iceberg of what He has put into place. Every good and beautiful creative work birthed on this earth is an expression and outflow of God. He is the source of all these things!

The swirling and ebbing of the ocean and the whizzing and spinning of the celestial bodies glorify God in their epic dance. In the same way, we humans assign glory to God just by doing what we were created to do. *All creation shouts out of the goodness and mercy and glory of God.*

Yet sometimes we miss the big picture. Rather than give thanks and praise to the Lord, we pride ourselves on our discoveries and progress. In fact, many have become so puffed up with a false sense of self-sufficiency, control, and importance that they reject the notion of their need for God and His existence altogether. They are blind and lack the perspective and wisdom to honor the God who is at work in and through and around them in every way. *Christ is supreme over all creation. He holds all things together.*

In Christ, "we live and move and have our being" (Acts 17:28), and He is worthy of all the glory and power and honor and praise in our hearts and lives. When we acknowledge God as the Reason and the Source of all good things and posture our hearts before Him in thanks, we deflect the glory to its rightful owner. In this way, He is exalted in the midst of our accomplishments. *Not to us, but to His name be the glory, because of His love and faithfulness.*

Embrace God's Word

For further insight, read Colossians 1:15-17; Psalm 115:1; Psalm 19:1; and Romans 1:20.

Journal Your Thoughts

What is one accomplishment in your life? Take time to practice assigning the praise to God.

All Who Are Victorious

To the one who is victorious, I will give the right to sit with me on my throne, just as I was victorious and sat down with my Father on his throne.

—Revelation 3:21

*T*he letters to the seven churches in Asia, which open the Book of Revelation, provide a stunning look into God's value system. He sees His church through the lens of obedience to what He has said, perseverance in trials, love for Him and one another, and holiness in the midst of a sinful world. We see that God uses these criteria to assess each church, and in a similar fashion, God will one day judge us as we stand before His throne in eternity.

On that day, those who are deemed victorious will be called forth and rewarded. And who are the victorious? It is those who have resisted the pull of sin and who have persevered in trials. It is those who have stood firm in faith and love, and those who have traded in their lives to follow Jesus, trusting God to give the victory.

And what will be their reward?

To the one who is victorious, Jesus will give the right to sit with Him on His throne. She (or he) will eat from the tree of life in the paradise of God.

The one who is victorious will not be hurt by the second death. She will eat of the manna that has been hidden away in heaven. She will be given a white stone, and on the stone will be engraved a new name that no one knows except her. She herself will be inscribed with a new name.

To the one who is victorious, God will give authority over all the nations. She will receive the same authority Jesus received from the Father. She will be given the morning star!

The one who is victorious will be clothed in white. Her name will never be erased from the Book of Life, and Jesus Christ Himself will announce before the Father that she belongs to Him.

The one who is victorious will become a pillar in the temple of God. She will never have to leave it. Christ will write His name on her, and she will be a citizen in the city of God.

When we exercise obedience to the very end, hold fast to our hope in trials, love the Lord our God with all our hearts, minds, soul, and strength, we are victorious. We have the power to do all these things—to our dying breath—only by the power of God in us.

May this hope guide us to throw off the world and follow Jesus. May it lead us to trust Him in suffering and to love sacrificially. May we live our lives out of the promise and hope of that day. May we fear God and possess the reverence to run after Him with abandon. May we understand the urgency, and may we stand firm in faith to the end.

Embrace God's Word

For further insight, read Revelation 2:7, 11, 17, 26-29; 3:5, 12, 21

Journal Your Thoughts

Are you living a life that is victorious?

How can you ruthlessly cut away sin and obey God completely so that you will be crowned victorious?

Friend of God

Don't you know that friendship with the world means enmity against God? Therefore, anyone who chooses to be a friend of the world becomes an enemy of God.

—James 4:4

Our Heavenly Father has given us a most profound title through Christ's atonement: friend of God. It is unimaginable that a holy, awesome, eternal, and infinite God would elevate flawed and finite humans to such a place of honor, but yet this is what He has done. Because of His great love for us, He has humbled himself to lift us up. If we think about this truth long enough, we might burst! It is too wonderful for words, and our minds cannot comprehend the glory and love and eternal significance wrapped up in the bestowal of this standing.

But, even so, many blindly run after the things of the world, trading the eternal riches God offers for a cheap, deceptive, empty substitute. When we do not fear God, we make it our aim to enjoy the world, not realizing that this very posturing *makes us an enemy of God*—not realizing that God jealously longs for us to be faithful to Him. In this way, we scorn the unbelievable gift extended by a righteous God.

Jesus says, "You are my friends if you do what I command" (John 15:14). Did you catch the *if*? There is a qualification to friendship with God; it is obedience. And what does Jesus command? He instructs us to *remain in the Father's love and to love one another.* He tells us to *produce fruit that will last.*

When we abandon *the pursuit of the desires, lusts, and pride of this life,* we put on instead the most wonderful of truths; great honor and eternal life will be our unmerited reward: "The world and its desires pass away, but whoever does the will of God lives forever" (1 John 2:17).

Embrace God's Word

For further insight, read John 15:9-17 and 1 John 2:15-17.

Journal Your Thoughts

Examine your heart. Are you a friend of God, or do you find yourself loving the world?

If the latter, ask God to help you cast aside this love for the world, fix your eyes on Jesus, and run to reach the heavenward goal.

"My Peace I Give You"

Peace I leave with you; my peace I give you. I do not give to you as the world gives. Do not let your hearts be troubled and do not be afraid.

—John 14:27

As those who follow Jesus, we have been given a profound gift. It is the treasure of divinely inspired, *perfect peace*. This peace is not the result of a trouble-free life, nor is it a product of the illusion that we are the ones in control. It does not stem from the likelihood that nothing bad will happen or get its power from the okayness of our present circumstances. This peace is much deeper and far-reaching. It is supernatural and rooted in eternity. This peace is an outflow of the Holy Spirit in us. It has nothing to do with context and everything to do with God's goodness. He is holy and loving and wise. His way is righteous and His purposes far exceed what we can comprehend.

To apprehend peace, we must relinquish our perceived control (we never had it anyway). We must look to heaven and put our hope in the Eternal God who holds not only our lives in His hands but also the entire scope of our existence. If we are anxious, worried, or fearful, we heed the words of Jesus, "Do not let your hearts be troubled and do not be afraid" (John 14:27). This is an instruction, and we must put energy into following it. This requires self-discipline. We make a choice to trust our Heavenly Father, and instead of trying to bridle outcomes with our anxiety, we make it our mission to live each day faithfully for His glory. We pray confidently for God's will, His provision, for safety, and for blessing, *presenting our requests to Him*, and then we resolve to trust and obey Him regardless of the result.

Knowing peace has to do with believing that God cares for us. It has to do with the recognition that this suffering, trouble, and pain is temporary— that the scope of reality and the faithfulness of God far exceed the stuff of our problems. Let us learn what it means to cast our cares on the infinitely strong shoulders of our God and trust Him, and in this way, we "may overflow with hope by the power of the Holy Spirit" (Romans 15:13)!

Embrace God's Word

For further insight, read Isaiah 26:3; Philippians 4:6; and 1 Peter 5:7.

Journal Your Thoughts

When have you been allowing yourself to stew and worry about a situation?

Give this situation fully to God and receive His peace. Resolve to exercise self-control as you divert your energy to prayer, and to exercise trust in God's goodness.

"You, Follow Me"

When Peter saw him, he asked, "Lord, what about him?"
Jesus answered, "If I want him to remain alive until I return,
what is that to you? You must follow me."

—John 21:21-22

$\mathcal{T}$he life Jesus is calling us to live is not one of comparison but of obedience. When we spend our time looking around and worrying about how our life stacks up against the lives of those around us, the unfortunate outcome is either pridefulness, fear, conceit, self-pity, jealousy, or discontentment. At best, we come away with a shallow form of gratitude that is based on the suffering of others, not on the goodness and faithfulness of God. Jesus is calling us to look to Him only.

After Jesus died, He appeared on the earth many times over the course of forty days. He showed proof of His resurrection, performed miracles, and gave encouragement and further instructions. During this time, Jesus offered redemption to His beloved disciple Peter. Peter had denied Jesus three times on the day of His arrest. So, three times Jesus asked Peter if he loved Him. When Peter said, "Yes," each time, Jesus responded, "Feed my sheep."

While they walked and talked, Jesus offered Peter a glimpse into the martyr's death he would one day experience. As Peter turned these things over in his mind, he saw another disciple in the distance. He asked, "What about him, Lord?"

Jesus's response was profound, and it has deep implications for our lives today: "If I want him to remain alive until I return, what is that to you? You follow me" (John 21:22).

So today, as we round out our *Heavenly Minded Mom* journey together, I want to leave you with this: God has given each one of us a calling that is beautifully simple, completely unique, and utterly eternal—*to follow Him.* We must do this in faith, regardless of what it costs and regardless of how it compares to the journey, calling, or expectation of anyone around us. Whether that means a "good life" or the way of suffering or something in between, may we follow Jesus gratefully with unswerving devotion.

Embrace God's Word

For further insight, read John 21:15-25; Ecclesiastes 12:13-14; and Psalm 106:1.

Journal Your Thoughts

How has this ninety-day journey changed you? How will you continue to grow?

Conclusion

*T*hroughout this journey I have offered many examples of futility in our world and pointed out the meaninglessness of all that happens under the sun. I have demonstrated thinking and seeing from an eternal perspective, and I have sought to cultivate renewed, heavenly meaning within our daily pursuits. My hope is that, through these ninety days of "perspective therapy," God has entered in and led you to a new way of seeing and living.

My prayer for you today is that you would continue allowing these truths to soak into every corner of your mind, heart, and spirit. *May you offer your body as a living sacrifice, poured out on God's altar, and take up your cross, forsaking your life. May you run the race marked out for you with perseverance. May you fix your eyes, heart, and hope on heaven,* and learn to *trust God in all things* and *walk in daily obedience.* Most of all, may you discover what it means to *love the Lord your God with all your heart, mind, soul, and strength,* and then to *love your neighbor as yourself* in joyful overflow.

May God's grace be upon all who love our Lord Jesus Christ with an undying love.

Embrace God's Word

For further insight, read Romans 12:1; Luke 14:27; Hebrews 12:1-2; Colossians 3:1-3; Proverbs 3:4-5; Matthew 22:18-19; and Ephesians 6:23.

Additional Resources

*W*hen we take the time to share what God is doing in our lives with others, our understanding will grow. Not only will we hear new insights, we will also develop our own thoughts and applications as we process and discuss them verbally in community with like-minded Christ followers. We will also remember and ingest a much higher percentage of what we have read when we take the time to talk it out.

For this reason, I want to ensure that you have the resources you need to make *Heavenly Minded Mom* work in a group setting. At the end of each devotion, you will find a thought question or series of questions. Prior to meeting, everyone should complete a handful of these devotions (perhaps five or seven) and write answers to each question in a separate notebook. Each participant should also take the time to read the Scriptures that accompany each day's reading. These questions and Scriptures will serve as your primary discussion guide. If everyone is prepared and willing to share, these will most likely fill your time. However, should you need supplemental questions to keep the discussion moving, I have created a simple list of discussion questions that will apply to any or all of the devotions in this book. Keep this list handy and pull from it weekly or as needed. Skip over any questions you feel your group has already answered naturally throughout the discussion.

Discussion Questions

1. What stood out to you in the devotions you read this week?
2. Are you struggling with anything that you have read?
3. Do you have questions about anything you read this week?
4. Which Scripture is stirring in you the most? Why?
5. What did you learn about God this week?
6. How are you seeing eternity in your everyday life?
7. What is one thing you will sacrifice to follow Jesus this week?
8. What is one action step you can take this week to store up treasures in heaven?
9. How can we pray for one another this week?

Understanding Ecclesiastes

Some of the core themes within this devotional are drawn from the Old Testament Book of Ecclesiastes. In Ecclesiastes, the Teacher expresses and expands upon the scope and meaning of life.

I have noticed that the Book of Ecclesiastes is often disregarded at first glance by Christians who do not understand it. But for those who take the time and care to mine this rich quarry for its priceless treasures, Ecclesiastes provides life-changing perspective.

Because I have included many references to Ecclesiastes throughout *Heavenly Minded Mom,* I would like to share a simple framework with you that I believe will shed light and context on this beautiful, poetic piece of Holy Scripture.

In order to sift through the Book of Ecclesiastes, it will be helpful to understand two things.

The first thing to know is that the writer of Ecclesiastes possessed great God-given wisdom. Based on the study of many scholars and the time frame, writing style, and clues given in the text, the authorship of this book is attributed to King Solomon. If you know much about Solomon's life, you know that early in his reign as king of Israel, God appeared to him in a dream. God told Solomon to ask for whatever he wanted, and it would be given to him. Solomon asked for a discerning heart with which to lead the people of Israel well. God was pleased with this request and granted him not only great wisdom, but also many other blessings for which Solomon did not ask.

This priceless gift allowed Solomon to lead Israel into great prosperity and peace. It also enabled him to observe truths about the world to a heightened degree.

Rather than setting aside the words of Ecclesiastes when we find them difficult to accept or understand, we should remember that Solomon's insight was divinely rooted. Also, we know that God is sovereign and intentional. The Book of Ecclesiastes was canonized both based on its own merit and according to the will of God. For each of these reasons, the observations of the Teacher are well worth considering.

The second thing to recognize when reading the Book of Ecclesiastes is that the writer did not know Jesus because Jesus had not yet come to earth. Although there existed many holy and mysterious prophecies of the coming Messiah, the details of salvation and life after death were not spelled out. Perhaps God wanted His people to trust Him without having all the information. Regardless of the reason, we see this uncertainty woven into Solomon's words throughout the Book of Ecclesiastes. And yet, we see that at the end of his deep musings, Solomon ultimately threw himself on God's mercy. He closed out all his reflections by concluding that the best anyone can do in this life is to fear God and obey His commands. That is where the only hope for purpose or lasting meaning lies. It hinges on future reward from a God who loves to bless His righteous ones.

Solomon drew conclusions based on three sources of input: his knowledge of what God had revealed about His plan up to this point in history, Solomon's keen observations about life, and the deep wisdom God had given him. Life "under the sun" refers to the things of the world. This is the examination of the world apart from the hope of salvation and eternal life. It is the world as it is seen, apart from spiritual realities.

As you read the Book of Ecclesiastes for yourself (and I hope you will!), you will see conflicting conclusions as Solomon's thoughts meander and develop in different ways. The Teacher is in a difficult struggle between the meaningless and futility of this death-bound life and the call of God to trust Him and obey.

It is good to see the meaninglessness of life apart from Christ because this stirs our longing for real hope and drives us to take action! But, as you read Ecclesiastes, remember that you know something and someone the Teacher did not know: Jesus. For a complete picture of truth, we must overlay Solomon's wise and desperate insights about life under the sun with the joy and hope of the gospel.

70393711R00126

Made in the USA
Middletown, DE
13 April 2018